Scholastic Aptitude
Vocabulary

by Joseph R. Orgel, Ph.D

Educators Publishing Service, Inc.,
Cambridge and Toronto

Copyright © 1958, 1977, 1983 by Joseph R. Orgel

ISBN 0-8388-0067-X

CONTENTS

PREFACE

Words are a prime tool in the educative process. More critically, they command immediate attention because they loom as a peremptory challenge to high school students at a point when their scores in an aptitude test in vocabulary may decide whether or not they will be admitted to college.

However, merely recognizing the face of a word or having "some idea" of what it means is not enough; more important is having the ability to appreciate words, to manipulate them, to sense their nuances and ambience. Every standard vocabulary test attempts to measure all these abilities. For this reason, *Scholastic Aptitude Vocabulary* provides both a preliminary list of key words and meanings chosen on the basis of the author's long experience with such tests, and a follow-up battery of practice aptitude tests in word recognition, meaning, and use. Each aptitude test in the book poses questions of a variety of types, all of which are designed to gauge verbal mastery, usage skills, and a refined sense of discrimination.

Scholastic Aptitude Vocabulary is divided into two sections: (a) an introductory list of one thousand basic words, and (b) a liberal number of aptitude tests in vocabulary to afford sufficient practice drill for the student to utilize and reinforce in his memory the vital words on the list. The planned utility of the book goes steps farther than a mere listing of words. Not only will these vocabulary tests prove helpful to secondary school students in the process of developing their word power and enriching their working vocabularies, but also will afford students practice and familiarity with the specific types of questions in common use in scholastic aptitude tests for college entrance. The test drills will spotlight deficiencies so that students can undertake remedial measures which will serve ultimately to help them perform commendably in these critical tests.

The lexicon in the first section of the book constitutes, as the Romans would say, *multum in parvo*, "much in a little space." The person who devised what has become known as "Basic English" was persuaded that if one knew only 800 basic English words, one would be in a position to cope with the language. What the author of *Scholastic Aptitude Vocabulary* has attempted to do is to select one thousand words which appear consistently on practically every college entrance vocabulary test. The basic meaning of each word is provided. These entries are simply worded to be readily comprehensible to the student and not to be as formidable as those given in an unabridged dictionary. To make the list especially fruitful for study and an incentive to further vocabulary enrichment, related forms, synonyms, and antonyms have been affixed to the definition so that the student will eventually come to possess a larder of more than 4000 vitalized words.

It should be pointed out that no two synonyms have exactly the same meaning. This is the beauty and the treasure of English words. There must be a reason for the existence of a current word, otherwise why add a new word if an old one will perform the same duty. For example, *slim* and *skinny* are synonyms, but what a whale of difference it would mean to a young woman if she were called the pejorative "skinny" instead of the flattering "slim." Each word in the language, especially a descriptive adjective, has a distinctive character. The student who embarks on an analysis of the 1000-word list should recognize the fact that few antonyms are perfect opposites, and that two synonyms are seldom exactly alike. What the addition of synonyms and antonyms does for the definitions listed in this book is to increase and sharpen the student's understanding as well as to suggest the aura around a defined word. Note in particular that besides listing and defining nearly every word in the battery of aptitude tests, the word list identifies a number of other words that reappear as common items in all aptitude tests. Besides the regular standbys, it includes words of recent popularity and currency, the vogue words, and others like *charisma, mystique, ambience*. Without a knowledge of such parvenu words, no student can adequately function in the upper levels of education or appreciatively understand the media offerings.

It should be noted here that the battery of aptitude tests and vocabulary provided in the second part of the book represents in essence a consummation of the intensive systematic study of the 1000-word list. Although the questions on all the follow-up aptitude tests are not the ones actually given by the College Entrance Examination Board, they do resemble them closely in the nature of the content, the difficulty of the questions, and the forms in which the questions are framed. The tests measure identical educational goals.

Scholastic Aptitude Vocabulary may be used independently or in conjunction with other texts in vocabulary in the secondary school curriculum. It is not in any sense a "cram book." The student should be keenly aware that there is no substitute for systematic study over long periods of time. The author is confident that if this book is used properly, it will give candidates for college entrance the kind of word study and preparation in test techniques which they need if they are to attain creditable scores on the College Entrance Examinations.

ONE THOUSAND KEY WORDS

Abbreviations and terms used in this word list:
n.-noun *v.*-verb *adj.*-adjective *adv.*-adverb *prep.*-preposition *part.*-participle *syn.*-synonym(s) *ant.*-antonym(s) *sing.*-singular *pl.*-plural *pejorative*-used in a disparaging sense *cf.*-compare

1. **ABATE** *v.* (*n.* abatement)—to lessen. *Syn. v.* diminish, slacken, recede, wane. *Ant. v.* increase, augment, accrue; *n.* increment.

2. **abdicate** *v.* (*n.* abdication)—to give up (as power, position). *Syn. v.* renounce, resign, forsake, relinquish. *Ant. v.* retain, assume.

3. **abet** *v.* (*n.* abettor)—to encourage; to aid (*pejorative*). *Syn. v.*

instigate, spur, foment, provoke, incite.

4. **abeyance** *n.*—a temporary suspension or postponement.

5. **abhor** *v.* (*n.* abhorrence, *adj.* abhorrent)—to detest. *Syn. v.* loathe, execrate; *adj.* revolting, despicable, repugnant; *n.* aversion, revulsion. *Ant. v.* fancy, relish, cherish, revere.

6. **abjure** *v.*—to disavow; to retract. *Syn. v.* recant, renege, repudiate, forswear.

7. **aboriginal** *adj.* (*n.* aborigine)—existing from the beginning. *Syn. adj.* primitive, primeval, primordial.

8. **abortive** *adj.*—cut short in development or completion.

9. **abound** *v.* (*adj.* abounding, *n.* abundance)—to exist plentifully. *Syn. v.* prevail (*adj.* prevalent); *adj.* copious, profuse, rampant, rife; *n.* plethora. *Ant. adj.* scarce; *n.* dearth.

10. **aboveboard** *adj.*—forthright; candid; frank. *Ant. adj.* sly, devious, insidious, underhanded, furtive, surreptitious.

11. **abridge** *v.* (*n.* abridgment)—to shorten. *Syn. v.* condense, curtail, retrench, abbreviate. *Ant. v.* elongate, amplify, swell, expand.

12. **abscond** *v.*—to depart secretly (for an evil purpose).

13. **academic** *adj.* (*n.* academician)—theoretical or unrealistic as opposed to practical; relating to an academy. *Syn. adj.* abstract, scholastic.

14. **accelerate** *v.* (*n.* acceleration)—to quicken. *Syn. v.* expedite (*adj.* expeditious), dispatch; *adj.* speedy. *Ant. v.* retard, decelerate, flag.

15. **accolade** *n.*—award; high praise or acclaim. *Syn. n.* ovation, kudos, homage, eulogy, panegyric; *v.* hail, laud. *Ant. v.* berate, stigmatize.

16. **accord** *v., n.* (*n.* accordance)—*v.* to grant or bestow; *n.* agreement. *Syn. n.* concord, amity, assent, consensus, harmony. *Ant. n.* discord, dissension, conflict, animosity; *v.* dissent.

17. **acme** *n.*—highest point or ultimate degree of achievement. *Syn. n.* peak, apex, crest, meridian, zenith, culmination. *Ant. n.* nadir, abyss.

18. **acquiesce** *v.* (*adj.* acquiescent, *n.* acquiescence)—to agree to; to yield. *Syn. v.* comply, accede, concede, comply with; capitulate. *Ant. v.* dissent, balk, rebuff, snub, spurn, repulse.

19. **acquit** *v.* (*n.* acquittal)—to free of guilt or obligation. *Syn. v.* absolve, vindicate, exonerate, exculpate, release. *Ant. v.* convict, inculpate.

20. **acrimony** *n.* (*adj.* acrimonious)—bitterness of tone or temper. *Syn. adj.* acrid, acerb, biting, caustic, mordant, astringent, incisive, sarcastic, trenchant. *Ant. n.* affability; *adj.* gentle, mild-mannered, bland.

21. **adage** *n.*—a familiar saying or commonly observed truth. *Syn. n.* maxim, aphorism, truism, saw, proverb (*adj.* proverbial—

commonplace).

22. **adjourn** *v.* (*n.* adjournment)—to formally end a meeting; to suspend consideration of a matter to another time or place. *Syn. v.* defer; disband. *Ant. v.* convoke, summon.

23. **adjudicate** *v.*—to pass formal judgment. *Syn. v.* arbitrate, referee, determine judicially.

24. **ad-lib** *v.* (*n.* ad-libber)—to speak without prior preparation. *Syn. v.* extemporize (*adj.* extemporaneous), improvise (*n.* improvisation); *adj.* and *adv.* impromptu.

25. **admonish** *v.* (*n.* admonition)—to mildly disapprove; to caution; to advise against. *Syn. v.* reprove, chide, reprehend, chasten; warn; counsel. *Ant. v.* approve, laud, commend.

26. **adorn** *v.* (*n.* adornment)—to add beauty to; to decorate. *Syn. v.* embellish, garnish, enhance, beautify, bedeck.

27. **adulation** *n.* (*adj.* adulatory)—excessive praise or flattery. *Syn. n.* exaltation, encomium, panegyric. *Ant. n.* disapprobation, depreciation, censure, reprimand.

28. **advent** *n.*—arrival; approach of an important event.

29. **adverse** *adj.* (*n.* adversity—unfortunate circumstances)—hostile, unfavorable. (*n.* adversary—opponent, antagonist). *Syn. adj.* inimical; antagonistic; loath. *Ant. adj.* amicable, favorable, congenial.

30. **advert** *v.*—to refer to; to comment about.

31. **advocate** *v.* (*n.* advocacy)—to give active support to a cause. *Syn. v.* espouse; plead for; *n.* proponent, champion, activist.

32. **aesthetic** *adj.*—characterized by beauty.

33. **affable** *adj.* (*n.* affability)—amiable, pleasant. *Syn. adj.* genial, cordial, gracious, civil, urbane. *Ant. adj.* insolent, surly, curt, brusque, uncouth.

34. **affectation** *n.* (*adj.* affected)—an assumed or artificial air; a pretentious display. *Syn. n.* pose, mannerism; insincerity.

35. **affliction** *n.* (*v.* afflict)—misfortune; great suffering. *Syn. n.* anguish, distress, tribulation, woe.

36. **affluent** *adj.* (*n.* affluence)—flourishing; prosperous. *Ant. adj.* indigent, needy, impecunious, poverty-stricken, destitute, deprived, disadvantaged; *n.* adversity.

37. **aftermath** *n.*—the by-product or outcome of a catastrophe. *Syn. n.* wake, consequence, result.

38. **agenda** *n.* (*sing.,* agendum)—items prescribed for consideration at a meeting.

39. **aggrandize** *v.* (*n.* aggrandizement)—to extend or increase in power, wealth, scope or greatness. *Syn. v.* magnify. *Ant. v.* reduce, curtail, minimize, diminish.

40. **aggregate** *v.*, *n.* (*n.* aggregation)—*v.* to lump together; *n.* a total amount. *Syn. v.* amalgamate, consolidate; *n.* cluster, agglomeration, congeries.

41. **aggression** *n.* (*adj.* aggressive, *n.* aggressor)—an unprovoked

attack upon another. *Syn. n.* encroachment, intrusion, infringement; *adj.* combative, pugnacious.

42. **agile** *adj.*—able to move fast; mentally alert. *Syn. adj.* fleet, nimble, brisk, lively. *Ant. adj.* lethargic, torpid, sluggish.

43. **agrarian** *adj.*—pertaining to farmers and agriculture.

44. **alias** *n.*—an assumed or adopted name; otherwise called. *Syn. n.* nickname, sobriquet, *nom de plume*, pseudonym. (**anonymous**—with no name attached). *Ant. n.* appellation.

45. **alienate** *v.* (*adj.* alien, *n.* alienation, *adj.* alienable)—to estrange; to provoke indifference. *Syn. v.* disunite; *adj.* irreconcilable. *Ant. v.* reconcile, unite, reconciliate (*n.* reconciliation); *adj.* inalienable.

46. **allay** *v.*—to relieve; to quiet down. *Syn. v.* palliate, placate, mitigate, appease, alleviate, assuage, pacify, propitiate. *Ant. v.* intensify, aggravate, excite.

47. **allude** *v.* (*n.* allusion, *adj.* allusive)—to refer to by indirection. *Syn. v.* insinuate, intimate, hint at; *n.* innuendo. *Ant. v.* aver, assert, allege, asseverate, affirm.

48. **altruistic** *adj.* (*n.* altruism)—characterized by unselfishness or interest in others. *Ant. adj.* egoistic, egocentric.

49. **amateur** *n.*—a participant in an activity solely as a pastime. (**amateurish** *adj.*—characterized by unprofessional skill) *Syn. n.* dabbler, dilettante, volunteer. *Ant. n.* connoisseur, professional, expert.

50. **ambiguous** *adj.* (*n.* ambiguity)—vague; capable of being interpreted in more than one way. *Syn. adj.* hazy, nebulous; equivocal. *Ant. adj.* unambiguous, explicit; unequivocal.

51. **amend** *v.* (*n.* amendment)—to make changes in. *Syn. v.* alter, modify. (**emend** *v.*—improve or correct by alterations; rectify.)

52. **amulet** *n.*—a charm, talisman.

53. **anachronistic** *adj.* (*n.* anachronism)—out of chronological order.

54. **analogy** *n.* (*adj.* analagous)—an apt or partial resemblance or comparison in one or more respects. *Syn. n.* similarity, correspondence.

55. **anarchy** *n.* (*adj.* anarchic)—utter lawlessness or social chaos. *syn. n.* pandemonium, bedlam.

56. **anathema** *n.* (*v.* anathematize)—a detestable person or object; a curse; a formal ecclesiastical excommunication. *Syn. n.* execration (*adj.* execrable); loathing; bane (*adj.* baneful). *Ant. n.* blessing.

57. **anecdote** *n.* (*adj.* anecdotal)—a short biographical detail or episode.

58. **animation** *n.* (*v.* animate, *adj.* animated)—characterized by life or vitality. *Syn. n.* liveliness, spirit, vivaciousness. *Ant. adj.* inanimate, inert; passive; lethargic, languid (*n.* languor).

59. **animus** *n.* (*n.* animosity)—an intense feeling of hostility or hatred. *Syn. n.* antipathy, enmity, antagonism; rancor, malice; *adj.* inimical. *Ant. adj.* amicable, congenial.

60. **annul** *v.* (*n.* annulment)—to cancel; to render inoperative. *Syn. v.* nullify, abrogate, invalidate, void. *Ant. v.* ratify, validate, confirm, corroborate.

61. **anthology** *n.*—a collection of selected writings.

62. **anticipate** *v.* (*adj.* anticipatory, *n.* anticipation)—to consider or act beforehand; to look forward to. *Syn. v.* obviate (render unnecessary by preventive measures); preclude, forestall, foresee; *n.* expectation. *Ant. v.* reminisce (look back).

63. **antidote** *n.*—a neutralizing agent to relieve an injurious influence or condition. *Syn. n.* counteractive, counterproductive, remedy, preventative.

64. **antiquated** *adj.* (*n.* antiquity, *adj.* antiquarian)—very old; ancient. *Syn. adj.* antediluvian (literally, "before the flood"), superannuated, obsolete, archaic. *Ant. adj.* novel, fashionable, contemporary.

65. **antithesis** *n.* (*adj.* antithetical)—an exact opposite or contradiction. **anomaly** *n.* (*adj.* anomalous)—an apparently self-contradictory statement or situation; deviation from the normal order or form. *Syn. adj.* deviant, irregular, incongruous, inconsistent. **paradox** *n.* (*adj.* paradoxical)—an inconsistency, incongruity.

66. **apocryphal** *adj.*—not genuine. *Syn. adj.* spurious, unauthentic, counterfeit, bogus.

67. **apostate** *n.* (*n.* apostasy)—one who deserts one's religion or party. *Syn. n.* convert, proselyte, defector (one who forsakes one's country), turncoat, renegade.

68. **appall** *v.* (*adj.* appalling)—to fill with terror, fear or astonishment. *Syn. v.* petrify, shock, astound, disconcert, dishearten, dismay. *Ant. v.* inspirit, exhilarate.

69. **apprehend** *v.* (*adj.* apprehensive)—to be uneasy or fearful of the future; to comprehend; to put under arrest. *Syn. v.* anticipate (with fear or pleasure); discern (*n.* discernment); seize.

70. **apprise** *v.*—to inform.

71. **apropos** *adj., adv., prep.*—*adj.* relevant to the subject being discussed; fitting; *prep.* with reference to; *adv.* incidentally, speaking of. *Syn. adj.* seemly, appropriate; pertinent; in order; *adv.* by the way. *Ant. adj.* irrelevant, inopportune.

72. **apt** *adj.* (*n.* aptness, *n.* aptitude)—likely; skilled; inclined. *Syn. adj.* deft, dexterous, adroit; prone; easily taught; relevant, meet. *Ant. adj.* inept (*n.* ineptitude, ineptness), gauche; irrelevant (**ambidextrous**—skilled in both hands).

73. **arbitrary** *adj.* (*v.* arbitrate)—prejudiced; partial. *Syn. adj.*

biased, partisan; despotic. *Ant. adj.* equitable, just, fair, impartial. (**arbiter** *n.*—a referee.)

74. **arid** *adj.* (*n.* aridness)—barren, dry (literally and figuratively); with little rainfall. *Syn. adj.* dull, jejune (uninteresting); parched. *Ant. adj.* fertile, fecund, lush.

75. **armistice** *n.*—a temporary suspension of hostilities by common consent. *Syn. n.* cease-fire; truce. *Ant. n.* combat, belligerency.

76. **aroma** *n.* (*adj.* aromatic)—a spicy or pleasant smell. *Syn. n.* redolence, fragrance, odor, scent, pungency.

77. **arrogant** *adj.* (*n.* arrogance, *v.* arrogate)—puffed up with pride of one's self-importance; bold and scornful in asserting importance. *Syn. adj.* overbearing, presumptuous, imperious, supercilious, haughty, contemptuous, disdainful, condescending. *Ant. adj.* meek, humble, modest, diffident.

78. **arson** *n.* (*n.* arsonist)—the malicious burning of property.

79. **articulate** *v.* and *adj.* (*n.* articulation)—to express firmly or clearly. *Syn. v.* enunciate; *adj.* well-coordinated (as a well-*articulated* mechanism); fluent. *Ant. adj.* inarticulate, incoherent; incomprehensible.

80. **artifice** *n.*—subtle or cunning trickery; craftiness. *Syn. n.* chicanery, ingenuity, stratagem, guile, duplicity.

81. **artless** *adj.*—without deceit or trickery. *Syn. adj.* naive (*n.* naivete), ingenuous, unsophisticated, guileless, innocent, unpretentious. *Ant. adj.* artful, guileful, devious, cunning, deceitful, subtle.

82. **askew** *adj.*—turned to one side. *Syn. adj.* awry, amiss (wrong), unsymmetrical. *Ant. adj.* balanced, proportioned, symmetrical.

83. **asperse** *v.* (*n.* aspersion)—to spread a malicious report. *Syn. v.* slander, vilify, revile, castigate, defame (*n.* defamation), malign, vituperate, calumniate.

84. **assiduous** *adj.* (*n.* assiduousness)—industrious. *Syn. adj.* diligent, studious, persevering, sedulous. *Ant. adj.* slothful, lazy, indolent, sluggard.

85. **astute** *adj.* (*n.* astuteness)—acutely perceptive. *Syn. adj.* shrewd, perspicacious (*n.* perspicacity), discerning, insightful, sagacious, canny, uncanny (extraordinarily skillful), sapient; *n.* acumen. *Ant. adj.* obtuse.

86. **asylum** *n.*—a refuge (*n.* refugee); a sheltering institution. *Syn. n.* haven.

87. **atonement** *n.* (*v.* atone)—amends for an offense or deficiency; regret or self-reproach for an action (or lack of it) or for a past sin. *Syn. n.* compunction, repentance (*v.* repent), penitence (*adj.* penitent), remorse (*adj.* remorseful), contrition (*adj.* contrite), expiation (*v.* expiate), reparation, conciliation; *v.* rue.

88. **atrocity** *n.* (*adj.* atrocious)—a cruel act. *Syn. adj.* outrageous (*n.* outrage), flagrant, heinous, nefarious, flagitious, monstrous; *n.* enormity. *Ant. n.* beneficence.

89. **auspicious** *adj.* (*n.* auspices—support or patronage)—marked by good fortune or expectation of future success. *Syn. adj.* propitious, fortuitous, providential, favorable. *Ant. adj.* ominous (exhibiting an omen suggesting misfortune), portentous.

90. **authoritative** *adj.*—official. **authoritarian** *adj.*—dictatorial, demanding total obedience. **autocracy** *n.* (*adj.* autocratic)— absolute rule by one person. *Syn. adj.* autocratic, despotic; *n.* absolutist, tyrant. *Ant. adj.* democratic, autonomous; *n.* constitutionalist.

91. **avarice** *n.* (*adj.* avaricious)—inordinate greed (especially for wealth). *Syn. n.* cupidity; *adj.* covetous.

92. **avid** *adj.* (*n.* avidity)—very enthusiastic. *Syn. adj.* ardent, zealous, covetous (*v.* covet—ardently desire), greedy, desirous, fervid.

93. **avocation** *n.* (*adj.* avocational)—a supplementary occupation in leisure; sideline. *Syn. n.* diversion, hobby.

94. **axiom** *n.* (*adj.* axiomatic)—a self-evident truth universally acknowledged. *Syn. n.* postulate.

95. **azure** *n.*—blue.

96. **BADGER** *v.*—to annoy or harry persistently by teasing, nagging or threatening. *Syn. v.* taunt, harass (*n.* harassment), bait.

97. **bagatelle** *n.*—a trifle.

98. **bait** *v.*—to lure with intent to entrap. *Syn. v.* allure, entice, seduce (*adj.* seductive); *v.* and *n.* decoy.

99. **balm** *n.*—something that comforts or soothes. *Syn. n.* solace.

100. **banter** *n.*—a light-hearted or good-natured verbal exchange; teasing; joshing. *Syn. n.* badinage, persiflage, raillery, sally, quip, repartee; touche.

101. **baroque** *adj.*—characterized in style by elaborate ornamentation. *Syn. adj.* flamboyant, rococo, showy, resplendent, ornate.

102. **bastion** *n.*—a fortified place. *Syn. n.* stronghold, bulwark, rampart(s). (**buttress** *v.*—to support or strengthen. *Syn. v.* prop, shore up).

103. **bawdy** *adj.*—humorously indecent. *Syn. adj.* ribald, risque, droll (comical, joking or amusing though not necessarily indecent).

104. **beget** *v.* (*past* **begat** or **begot**, *past part.* **begotten**)—to produce; bring about. *Syn. v.* engender, burgeon, reproduce; *n.* genesis. *Ant. v.* blight, raze (level).

105. **bellicose** *adj.* (*n.* bellicosity)—of a quarreling disposition. *Syn. adj.* quarrelsome, pugnacious, militant, martial, disputatious, contentious. *Ant. adj.* pacific, pacifist.

106. **benediction** *n.*—a blessing. *Syn. n.* benison. *Ant. n.* malediction

(slander, calumny), imprecation, execration, anathema.

107. **benevolent** *adj.* (*n.* benevolence)—doing good; generous. *Syn. adj.* bountiful, beneficent (*n.* beneficence), munificent, magnanimous; *n.* benefactor (*n.* benefaction). *Ant. adj.* malevolent (*n.* malevolence), malignant, malicious, pernicious.

108. **benign** *adj.* (*adj.* benignant)—displaying kindness or gentleness; tending to foster well-being. *Syn. adj.* beneficial, mild; non-injurious. *Ant. adj.* malignant.

109. **bereaved** *adj.*—grief-stricken, especially by another's death. **bereft** *adj.*—deprived of (hope, a beloved one); left destitute (by death).

110. **berserk** *adj.*—enraged and violently destructive. *Syn. adj.* demented (insane).

111. **biased** *adj.* (*n.* bias)—prejudiced. *Syn. adj.* bigoted (*n.* bigot, bigotry), partial, arbitrary intolerant. *Ant. adj.* impartial, nonpartisan, tolerant.

112. **bibliophile** *n.*—a lover of books; book-collector. *Ant. n.* bibliophobe.

113. **bicker** *v.*—to quarrel in a petty way. *Syn. v.* (not necessarily petty) squabble, brawl, wrangle.

114. **bizarre** *adj.*—strange in manner and/or appearance. *Syn. adj.* odd, outlandish, grotesque, exotic, freakish, eccentric. *Ant. adj.* stylish, fashionable, chic.

115. **bland** *adj.*—mild; lackluster; dull. *Syn. adj.* suave, non-irritating. *Ant. adj.* irritating, caustic, corrosive; piquant, racy.

116. **blase** *adj.*—bored with life or surfeited by overindulgence. *Syn. adj.* insouciant (pretentiously), sophisticated; *n.* ennui (boredom).

117. **blatant** *adj.* (*n.* blatancy)—conspicuously noisy; obvious. *Syn. adj.* clamorous, vociferous, boisterous (rowdy, unruly), obstreperous, rambunctious. *Ant. adj.* dulcet, mild-mannered.

118. **bleak** *adj.* (*n.* bleakness)—desolate; cheerless. *Syn. adj.* depressing, raw, grim, forbidding, dismal, dreary, drab. *Ant. adj.* cozy (snug), promising.

119. **bliss** *n.* (*adj.* blissful, *n.* blissfulness)—exalted, happiness. *Syn. n.* felicity (*adj.* felicitous). *Ant. adj.* somber, depressing.

120. **blithe** *adj.* (*adj.* blithesome)—cheerful. *Syn. adj.* gay, joyous, buoyant, sprightly, mirthful, jovial, jubilant, convivial, jocular. *Ant. adj.* disconsolate, melancholy, morose, dismal, solemn, sullen, gloomy, dour, doleful, dolorous, downhearted, depressed, dejected.

121. **blunt** *adj.*—curt or abrupt in manner or speech. *Syn. adj.* brusque, brash, burly, gruff. *Ant. adj.* urbane, civil.

122. **bog** *n.*—a swamp. *Syn. n.* morass, fen, marsh, mire.

123. **bombastic** *adj.* (*n.* bombast)—high-flown or inflated in language. *Syn. adj.* fustian, grandiloquent, turgid, pretentious, pompous. *Ant. adj.* concise, succinct, prosaic.

124. **bowdlerize** *v.*—to purge a book, article or other objectionable passages. *Syn. v.* purify; censor.

125. **braggadocio** *n.*—pretentious boasting. *Syn. n.* bravado (false courage), bluster, cockiness, rodomontade, bragging, swagger.

126. **breach** *n.*—a gap or break; a violation. *Syn. n.* schism (ideological split in the ranks of a party), lacuna, hiatus, cleft; infraction, transgression, trespass.

127. **bucolic** *adj.*—characteristic of the countryside. *Syn. adj.* pastoral, rural, rustic. *Ant. adj.* urban, metropolitan.

128. **buffoon** *n.* (*n.* buffoonery)—a clown. *Syn. n.* jester, harlequin.

129. **CABAL** *n.*—a small band of conspirators. *Syn. n.* faction, clique, junta, junto.

130. **cacophonous** *adj.* (*n.* cacophony)—harsh and discordant in sound. *Syn. adj.* dissonant, raucous, grating, strident. *Ant. adj.* euphonious, melodious, sonorous, dulcet.

131. **capricious** *adj.* (*n.* capriciousness, *n.* caprice)—fickle, whimsical, changeable. *Syn. adj.* temperamental, inconstant, flighty, impulsive.

132. **captious** *adj.*—given to petty fault-finding. *Syn. adj.* caviling, carping.

133. **careen** *v.*—to dip to one side. *Syn. v.* lurch, sway.

134. **caricature** *n.*—a pictorial, exaggerated distortion in the representation of a person (group, people) in order to poke fun at or to satirize a characteristic peculiarity or mannerism. *Syn. n.* burlesque (a ludicrous imitation of a literary composition), parody.

135. **carmine** *n.*—a purplish-red color.

136. **cartel** *n.*—an international combination of businesses organized to regulate production and marketing of products and thus to fix or regulate prices. *Syn. n.* combination, conglomerate, monopoly.

137. **catastrophe** *n.*(*adj.* catastrophic)—a complete collapse. *Syn. n.* collapse, cataclysm (*adj.* cataclysmic), disaster, fiasco, rout, debacle (sudden violent collapse).

138. **caucus** *n.*—a meeting of party leaders to decide on a unified policy or choice of candidates.

139. **celestial** *adj.*—heavenly, divine; pertaining to the sky.

140. **censor** *v.* (*n.* censorship, *adj.* censorable)—to examine and suppress the objectionable parts of a speech, exhibit, motion picture, or literary work on moral, political, or other grounds. (*adj.* **censorious**—severely critical; expressing censure.) *Syn. v.* expurgate, delete, expunge, excise, purge.

141. **censure** *v.* (*adj.* censurable)—criticize adversely. *Syn. v.* condemn (*n.* condemnation), disapprove (*n.* disapprobation), reprehend, denounce (*n.* denunciation), reprove. *Ant. v.* approve, sanction; praise.

142. **chagrin** *n.*—a mental upset stemming from keen disappointment or humiliation. *Syn. n.* mortification; *adj.* abashed. *Ant. n.* jubilation, exultation, rapture.

143. **charitable** *adj.*—generous in giving help or in passing judgment. *Syn. adj.* eleemosynary; philanthropic; tolerant; lenient.

144. **charlatan** *n.* (*n.* charlatanry)—an imposter. *Syn. n.* fraud, humbug, mountebank, quack, faker; *adj.* bogus.

145. **chauvinist** *n.* (*adj.* chauvinistic, *n.* chauvinism)—a fanatically patriotic person. *Syn. n.* patrioteer, nationalist.

146. **chimerical** *adj.*—extravagantly visionary or unreal. *Syn. adj.* fanciful, fantastic, utopian. *Ant. adj.* pragmatic, sensible, reasonable.

147. **chronic** *adj.*—long-lasting; constantly recurrent. *Syn. adj.* eternal, inveterate, continuous. *Ant. adj.* infrequent, ephemeral, transitory, sporadic, occasional.

148. **circumspect** *adj.* (*n.* circumspection)—cautious. *Syn. adj.* prudent, guarded, chary, wary. *Ant. adj.* rash, imprudent.

149. **circumvent** *v.*—to secure an advantage through clever maneuvering or bypassing; to outwit; to go round. *Syn. v.* frustrate, elude; *adj.* circuitous.

150. **clamor** *n.* (*adj.* clamorous)—a loud outcry, as of distress, demand, or protest. *Syn. n.* hubbub, din, uproar; *adj.* vociferous, stentorian, blaring.

151. **clandestine** *adj.*—secretive, usually for a sinister purpose. *Syn. adj.* furtive, covert, surreptitious. *Ant. adj.* conspicuous, salient, overt.

152. **clarify** *v.* (*n.* clarification, *n.* clarity)—to make clear. *Syn. v.* elucidate, enlighten. *Ant. v.* obscure, obfuscate.

153. **claustrophobia** *n.* (*adj.* claustrophobic)—morbid fear of enclosed places. **agoraphobia** *n.*—fear of open spaces. **acrophobia** *n.*—fear of high places. **gynephobia** *n.*—fear of women.

154. **cliché** *n.*, *adj.*—(a) *n.* a commonplace thing or expression; (b) *adj.* outworn through overuse; hence, unoriginal. *Syn. n.* (a) bromide, platitude. *adj.* (b) trite, hackneyed, stereotyped, platitudinous, banal (*n.* banality).

155. **coalesce** *v.* (*adj.* coalescent, *n.* coalition)—to merge. (**coalition** *n.*—a temporary union of heads of different political parties.) *Syn. v.* integrate, fuse (*n.* fusion), amalgamate, consolidate, blend; *n.* confederation, union. *Ant. v.* disunite, sunder, cleave, splinter, fragment, disintegrate, segregate; *n.* disunion, schism, separatism, secession.

156. **cogent** *adj.* (*n.* cogency)—strongly persuasive. *Syn. adj.* incisive, pungent, forceful, convincing.

157. **colloquy** *n.*—a conference of, or conversation between, two or more persons. **soliloquy** *n.*—a monolog. **colloquial** *adj.*— informal or conversational in language. **colloquialism** *n.*—a colloquial expression. **colloquium** *n.*—a formal study discussion conference.

158. **collude** *v.* (*n.* collusion, *adj.* collusive)—secretly to conspire to defraud. *Syn. v.* connive, plot, intrigue; *n.* cabal, machination.

159. **colossal** *adj.*—enormous in size, degree, or extent. *Syn. adj.* immense, imposing, prodigious, massive, gigantic, titanic, stupendous, gargantuan, mammoth. *Ant. adj.* picayune, lilliputian, diminutive. (**enormity** *n.*—an outrage; excessive wickedness.)

160. **commit** *v.* (*n.* commitment, *n.* committal)—(a) to perform; (b) to entrust; (c) to consign (to a person). **commitment** *n.*—a pledge to perform something. *Syn. v.* (a) perpetrate, (b) delegate, (c) relegate.

161. **commodious** *adj.*—roomy. *Syn. adj.* spacious.

162. **compact** *adj.*, *n.* (*n.* compactness)—(a) *adj.* firmly packed; (b) *n.* a formal alliance; (c) *adj.* condensed (said of language). *Syn.* (b) *n.* entente, concordat, covenant, pact; (c) *adj.* succinct, terse, pithy, sententious. *Ant.* (b) *n.* dissension, discord; (c) *adj.* diffuse.

163. **compassion** *n.* (*adj.* compassionate)—sympathy for, or sharing in, another's suffering. *Syn. n.* concern, commiseration, condolence, empathy; *v.* condole. *Ant. adj.* dispassionate, callous, insensitive, indifferent.

164. **compatible** *adj.* (*n.* compatibility)—congenial, harmonious. *Ant. adj.* irreconcilable, discordant.

165. **compendium** *n.* (*adj.* compendious)—a brief summary of subject. *Syn. n.* epitome, digest, resume, precis. *Ant. adj.* encyclopedic.

166. **comprehend** *v.* (*adj.* comprehensive, *adj.* comprehensible, *n.* comprehension)—(a) to understand; (b) to include. *Syn. v.* (a) grasp, apprehend; (b) comprise, encompass.

167. **concise** *adj.* (*n.* conciseness)—expressed briefly. *Syn. adj.* incisive, succinct, to the point, terse, pithy. *Ant. adj.* diffuse, verbose, prolix, turgid, redundant (superfluous), tautological.

168. **condone** *v.*—to extenuate (excuse); to pardon. *Syn. v.* forgive, overlook (an offense). *Ant. v.* censure, decry.

169. **confederate** *n.* (*n.* confederation, *n.* confederacy)—an ally; an accomplice (*pejorative*), as in a plot. *Syn. n.* associate, colleague.

170. **conflagration** *n.*—a big fire. *Syn. n.* holocaust.

171. **consecrate** *v.* (*n.* consecration)—to render or declare sacred. *Syn. v.* hallow, sanctify; dedicate. *Ant. v.* desecrate (*n.* desecra-

tion), profane (*n.* profanation).

172. **constitute** *v.* (*n.*, *adj.* constituent, *n.* constituency)—to compose or make up of elements. **constituent** *n.*—a component part; one represented by an elected official.

173. **contempt** *n.* (*v.* contemn)—scorn. **contemptible** *adj.*—detestable. *Syn. adj.* despicable. **contemptuous** *adj.*—scornful; disdainful. **contumelious** *adj.*—using insulting scornful language. *Ant. n.* graciousness, civility; deference.

174. **contiguous** *adj.* (*n.* contiguity)—near. *Syn. adj.* adjacent, adjoining.

175. **contingent** *adj.*—dependent; conditional. **contingency** *n.*—a possible event; a likelihood. *Syn. n.* future uncertainty.

176. **contravene** *v.* (*n.* contravention)—to argue in opposition; to violate; to breach (an agreement). *Ant. v.* uphold.

177. **contretemps** *n.*—an embarrassing or inconvenient mishap.

178. **convoke** *v.* (*n.* convocation)—to summon to a meeting.

179. **corpulent** *adj.* (*n.* corpulence)—fat. *Syn. adj.* obese (*n.* obesity), stocky, paunchy, stout (robust), portly. *Ant. adj.* lean, gaunt, emaciated, slim, slender.

180. **cosmopolitan** *adj.*—(a) worldly-wise; (b) free of local or national prejudices. *Syn. adj.* (a) sophisticated, urbane, polished; savoir-faire. *Ant. adj.* (a) unsophisticated, boorish, uncouth, crude. (b) parochial, insular, provincial, narrow-minded, bigoted.

181. **countenance** *n.*, *v.*—(a) *n.* face, aspect, appearance; (b) *v.* to approve, to tolerate. *Syn.* (a) *n.* visage, (b) *v.* sanction.

182. **coup** *n.*—a masterly blow or attack. **coup d'etat**—a sudden forcible and illegal overthrow of an existing government.

183. **crass** *adj.*—grossly stupid, coarse.

184. **craven** *adj.*—cowardly. *Syn. adj.* dastardly, recreant. *Ant. adj.* intrepid, dauntless, undaunted, fearless, mettlesome, valiant, gallant, doughty, plucky.

185. **creed** *n.* (*n.* credo)—a doctrine; a system of beliefs. **credence** *n.*—belief, validity. **credulous** *adj.*—readily inclined to believe anything; hence, easily imposed upon. *Syn. adj.* gullible. **credible** *adj.*— (*n.* credibility) plausible; believable. *Ant. adj.* incredible. **creditable** *adj.*—trustworthy. *Ant. adj.* discreditable.

186. **crescendo** *n.*—gradual increase in loudness or intensity.

187. **cringe** *v.*—to shrink back or acquiesce out of fear or alarm. *Syn. v.* cower, quail, recoil, flinch; fawn, kowtow; *adj.* obsequious.

188. **criterion** *n.* (*pl.*, criteria)—a standard of judgment.

189. **crucial** *adj.*—critical; decisive. *Syn. adj.* momentous.

190. **culpable** *adj.* (*n.* culpability)—guilty; blameworthy. *Syn. adj.* censurable. (**culprit** *n.*—an offender; a person guilty of a fault or crime.)

191. **cult** *n.* (*n.* cultist, *n.* cultism)—an exclusive group or sect venerat-

ing a person, idea, practice or tradition. *Syn. n.* fad, craze.

192. **curb** *v.* —to check. *Syn. v.* repress, restrain, inhibit, block, stifle, bridle.

193. **cursory** *adj.* —hasty. *Syn. adj.* superficial, perfunctory. *Ant. adj.* thorough, meticulous.

194. **cynic** *n.*(*adj.* cynical, *n.* cynicism) – one who believes that people are basically selfish.

195. **cynosure** *n.* —the center of attraction.

196. **DAIS** *n.* —a platform above the floor of a hall or large room. *Syn. n.* podium, rostrum, pulpit.

197. **dapper** *adj.* —smartly dressed; trim. *Syn. adj.* neat, elegant; dashing (stylish, gallantly audacious). *Ant. adj.* untidy, slovenly, shabby, dowdy, unkempt, frowzy, disheveled.

198. **daub** *v.* —to spread over or cover with paint, plaster, etc. *Syn. v.* smear.

199. **daunt** *v.* (*adj.* daunted)—to overcome with fear or anxiety. *Syn. v.* faze, dishearten, cow, intimidate, dismay; *n.* consternation. *Ant. adj.* dauntless, undismayed, fearless.

200. **deadlock** *n.* —a standstill caused by refusal of contending parties in a dispute to budge. *Syn. n.* stalemate, impasse.

201. **dearth** *n.* —scarcity. *Syn. n.* paucity, shortage; sparseness. *Ant. n.* plethora (*adj.* plethoric), profusion, redundance, glut, copiousness.

202. **debilitate** *v.* (*adj.* debilitated)—to weaken; to enfeeble. *Syn. v.* enervate; wear out; *n.* impairment.

203. **debonair** *adj.* —pleasant in manner; gay. *Syn. adj.* sprightly, affable, gracious, insouciant, suave, jaunty. *Ant. adj.* rude, crude, ungracious, surly.

204. **decorum** *n.* (*adj.* decorous)—propriety; proper behavior. *Syn. n.* protocol, etiquette. *Ant. n.* impropriety, breach (of etiquette).

205. **decrepit** *adj.* (*n.* decrepitude)—infirm; feeble; in disrepair. *Syn. n.* decay, deterioration, decadence. *Ant. adj.* vigorous.

206. **defeatist** *n.* (*n.* defeatism)—one who feels that defeat is inevitable or that resistance is futile.

207. **defer** *v.* (*adj.* deferred)—(a) to postpone; (b) to yield out of respect or consideration of another's wishes, age or authority. *Syn.* (a) *v.* procrastinate. *Ant.* (b) *v.* disdain, spurn, snub, slight. (**deferment** *n.* —temporary exemption from military service.) (**deference** *n.* (*adj.* deferential)—accession; (respectful) submission; regard; compliance.)

208. **definitive** *adj.* —all-conclusive, comprehensive, as "a *definitive* edition."

209. **defunct** *adj.* —no longer functioning. *Syn. adj.* extinct, effete. *Ant. adj.* extant.

210. **deign** *v.* —to stoop in position before an inferior person. *Syn. v.* condescend, patronize.

211. **delectable** *adj.* (*n.* delectation)—highly pleasing; delicious. *Syn. adj.* enjoyable, delightful; savory, luscious. *Ant. adj.* distasteful, unpalatable, unsavory.

212. **delinquent** *adj.* (*n.* delinquency)—neglectful of duty or obligation; remiss. (**derelict** *n.* dereliction)—a person who is not a responsible or acceptable member of society, as in "a juvenile *delinquent.*") *Ant. adj.* punctilious (careful in meeting an obligation).

213. **delude** *v.* (*n.* delusion, *adj.* delusory)—to mislead; to deceive. *Syn. v.* defraud (*n.* fraudulent), cozen, beguile, dupe, hoodwink.

214. **demagogue** *n.* (*adj.* demagogic, *n.* demagoguery)—an unprincipled leader of the masses who stirs them up to satisfy his own objective. *Syn. n.* rabble-rouser, agitator, ringleader.

215. **demeanor** *n.*—behavior. *Syn. n.* deportment, bearing. **misdemeanor** *n.*—an offense less serious than a felony. **demean** *v.*—to debase or lower in dignity or position.

216. **demur** *v.*—to take exception; to offer objections because of one's scruples.

217. **denote** *v.* (*n.* denotation)—to refer to explicitly; to indicate or signify. *Syn. v.* characterize; *adj.* explicit. *Ant. v.* allude, hint at; *adj.* implicit.

218. **denouement** *n.*—the outcome or final solution of a plot or sequence of events.

219. **deny** *v.* (*n.* denial)—to contradict; to reject or refuse. *Syn. v.* gainsay, negate; withhold; disavow; refute. *Ant. v.* reiterate; affirm, aver.

220. **depraved** *adj.* (*n.* depravity)—morally perverted; unscrupulous.

221. **deprecate** *v.* (*adj.* deprecatory)—to disapprove vigorously; protest or plead against. *Syn. v.* deplore, expostulate, remonstrate (*n.* remonstrance). *Ant. v.* advocate.

222. **depreciate** *v.* (*adj.* depreciating, *n.* depreciation)—to belittle; to minimize; to undervalue. *Syn. v.* disparage, denigrate, derogate, detract, decry. *Ant. v.* flatter, adulate.

223. **deracinate** *v.* (*n.* deracination)—to isolate a person from his native culture or environment. *Syn. v.* alienate, extirpate. (**genocide** *n.*—the eradication of a whole nation or culture.)

224. **deride** *v.* (*adj.* derisive, *n.* derision)—to poke fun in contempt; scorn. *Syn. v.* ridicule, jeer at, gibe, scoff, disdain (*adj.* disdainful).

225. **desiccate** *v.* (*adj.* desiccated)—to dry thoroughly; (figuratively) dull. *Syn. adj.* dull, arid, spiritless, jejune, vapid. *Ant. adj.* sapid.

226. **destructive** *adj.* (*adj.* destructible)—harmful to excess. *Syn. adj.* noxious, deleterious, pernicious, detrimental, injurious, hazardous, perilous, baneful. *Ant. adj.* innocuous (harmless); salutary, salubrious, beneficial.

227. **desultory** *adj.*—rambling from subject to subject; aimless. *Syn.*

adj. discursive, unmethodical, fitful, haphazard.

228. **detente** *n.*—the relaxation of tension (usually between nations).

229. **deviate** *v.* (*n.* deviation, *n.* deviant)—(a) to turn from a course of action; (b) to depart from prescribed normal behavior. *Syn.* (a) *v.* digress (*adj.* digressive, *n.* digression), veer, diverge, swerve, err, stray. (b) *adj.* abnormal. (**devious** *adj.*— underhanded, shifty.) (**deviant** *n.*—a pervert.)

230. **devilish** *adj.* (*n.* deviltry—gross mischief)—relating to the devil. *Syn. adj.* diabolical, fiendish, satanic.

231. **devoid** *adj.*—lacking in; empty, deficient. *Syn. adj.* depleted, bereft, destitute. *Ant. adj.* replete, fraught, copious.

232. **devout** *adj.* (*n.* devoutness; *adj.* devotional)—religiously observant. *Syn. adj.* pious, faithful (in a religious sense). *Ant. adj.* unobservant, irreligious.

233. **diagnosis** *n.* (*v.* diagnose, *adj.* diagnostic, *n.* diagnostician)—the art or act of recognizing the nature of a condition (like disease) by careful examination. *Syn. n.* analysis.

234. **dialogue** *n.*—a conversation between two or more persons; an exchange of ideas or opinions in order to erase misunderstanding (vogue meaning). **monolog** *n.* (*n.*monologist)–a soliloquy (*v.* soliloquize) or an utterance aloud by one to oneself. **parley** *n.*–a conference between enemies to discuss truce terms.

235. **dichotomy** *n.*—division into two opposing or contradictory units, parts, opinions. *Syn. n.* schism, split.

236. **dicker** *v.*—to trade by petty bargaining. *Syn. v.* haggle, higgle.

237. **didactic** *adj.* (*n.* didacticism)—intended for formal or moral instruction; inclined to excessive teaching or preaching. *Syn. n.* moralism; pedagogy (*adj.* pedagogical).

238. **diffuse** *v.*—to disseminate. *Syn. v.* spread, scatter, disperse. *Ant. adj.* concise, succinct. **diffusive** *adj.* (*n.* diffusiveness)— rambling, desultory.

239. **dire** *adj.*—dreadful; causing disaster. *Syn. adj.* calamitous.

240. **disarming** *adj.*—moving to dispel suspicion or animosity.

241. **disburse** *v.* (*n.* disbursement)—to pay out. *Syn. v.* expend.

242. **disclaim** *v.*—to disown. *Syn. v.* repudiate, disavow (*n.* disavowal), renounce (*n.* renunciation).

243. **discourse** *n.*—conversation; extended treatment of a subject in speech or writing. *Syn. n.* treatise, disquisition, dissertation.

244. **discreet** *adj.* (*n.* discreetness, *n.* discretion, *adj.* discretionary)— good judgment; cautious in action or judgment; prudent. *Syn. adj.* judicious. *Ant. adj.* indiscreet, injudicious, imprudent.

245. **discriminate** *v.* (*adj.* discriminatory, *n.* discrimination, *adj.* discriminative)—(a) to make or recognize fine or acute distinctions and judgments. *Syn. n.* perspicacity, acumen,

insight. (b) to use favoritism or prejudice in treating persons or making decisions. *Syn. adj.* prejudicial, biased. (**indiscriminate** *adj.*—haphazard, wanton.)

246. **disfranchise** *v.* (*n.* disfranchisement)—to deprive of citizenship. *Ant. v.* emancipate, liberate.

247. **disillusion** *v.* (*n.* disillusionment)—to free from an erroneous impression. *Syn. v.* disenchant. *Ant. v.* delude, deceive, hoodwink, dupe, bamboozle (informal).

248. **disinter** *v.*—to dig up. *Ant. v.* inter.

249. **disparity** *n.* (*adj.* disparate)—a lack of similarity or equality. *Syn. n.* incongruity; *adj.* discrete, dissimilar. *Ant. n.* parity, congruence, similitude.

250. **disposition** *n.*—a tendency; temperament. *Syn. n.* trend, inclination, leaning, predilection, predisposition, proclivity, propensity. *Ant. n.* disinclination, aversion.

251. **dissipate** *v.* (*n.* dissipation)—(a) to scatter (b) to live intemperately; to squander (spend recklessly). *Syn.* (a) *v.* dispel, disperse, rout. (b) *adj.* profligate (*n.* profligacy), dissolute, intemperate.

252. **distraught** *adj.*—deeply distressed or anguished, disconsolate.

253. **diurnal** *adj.*—daily.

254. **divers** *adj.*—several.

255. **diverse** *adj.* (*v.* diversify, *n.* diversity)—varied. *Syn. adj.* disparate.

256. **divert** *v.* (*adj.* diverting, *n.* diversion)—(a) to entertain; to amuse. (b) to turn aside. *Syn.* (a) *v.* regale, distract, relax. (b) *v.* deflect, deviate, diverge (*adj.* divergent), vary. (**divertissement** *n.*—an amusement or entertainment.)

257. **divulge** *v.*—to reveal or disclose a secret.

258. **doctrinaire** *n.*—a zealous, dogmatic advocate of an impractical doctrine.

259. **doff** *v.*—to discard or throw away. *Ant. v.* don.

260. **dogmatic** *adj.* (*n.* dogmatism)—arrogantly highly opinioned; stubborn in asserting one's views. *Syn. adj.* overbearing, authoritarian (see **doctrinaire**). (**dogma** *n.*—a system of religious doctrines or beliefs.)

261. **dormant** *adj.* (*n.* dormancy)—inactive; temporarily suspended in development. *Syn. adj.* inert, latent, hibernating, quiescent. *Ant. adj.* potent, lively.

262. **dotage** *n.* (*v.* dote)—feeble-mindedness due to old age. *Syn. n.* senility.

263. **dovish** *adj.*—favoring a peace policy in foreign affairs. *Ant. adj.* hawkish.

264. **dross** *n.*—waste-matter; refuse.

265. **duress** *n.*—restraint. *Syn. n.* constraint, coercion.

266. **EBB** *v.*—to decrease or decline slowly. *Syn. v.* recede (*n.* recession), diminish, evanesce (*n.* evanescent). *Ant. v.* wax,

accrue, augment.

267. **ebullient** *adj.* (*n.* ebullience, *n.* ebullition)—overflowing with high spirits. *Syn. adj.* effervescent, exuberant, vivacious. *Ant. adj.* sober, unruffled, imperturbable.

268. **ecclesiastic** *adj.* (*adj.* ecclesiastical)—relating to the church. *Syn. adj.* ministerial, churchly. *Ant. adj.* secular (worldly); *n.* layman; laity.

269. **echelon** *n.*—rank of authority or power.

270. **eclat** *n.*—brilliance or dazzling effect, as of performance or success.

271. **eclectic** *adj.*—chosen from the best of various sources. *Syn. adj.* selective.

272. **ecology** *n.* (*adj.* ecological, *n.* ecologist)—the biological science dealing with the relationships between environment and living organisms.

273. **ecstasy** *n.* (*adj.* ecstatic)—extraordinary joy or delight. *Syn. n.* rapture, exultation, transport, elation. *Ant. n.* despondency, dejection, despondence.

274. **ecumenical** *adj.* (*n.* ecumenicalism)—relating to the church; universal; world-wide.

275. **edict** *n.*—an official order or proclamation. *Syn. n.* dictum, fiat.

276. **edify** *v.* (*n.* edification)—to enlighten spiritually; to instruct; to improve and elevate.

277. **efface** *v.* (*n.* effacement)—to wipe out completely. *Syn. v.* obliterate, eradicate, extirpate, expunge, raze, level. *Ant. v.* rear, engender.

278. **efficacious** *adj.* (*n.* efficacy, *adj.* effectual, *v.* effectuate)—highly effective. *Ant. adj.* inefficacious, ineffective, fruitless, futile, feckless, effete.

279. **effrontery** *n.*—shameless or impudent boldness. *Syn. n.* audacity, temerity. *Ant. adj.* timorous (shy, full of fear).

280. **egalitarian** *n.*—an advocate of equal rights for all citizens.

281. **egotistic** *adj.* (*n.* egotist, *adj.* egotistical, *n.* egotism; *n.* ego, *n.* egoist, *n.* egoism)—conceited; given to boastfulness or to self-admiration. *Syn. adj.* selfish, vain, egocentric, narcissistic. *Ant. adj.* altruistic, modest, meek.

282. **egregious** *adj.*—outstanding or extraordinary (*pejorative*). *Syn. adj.* notorious, conspicuous, prominent, exceptional.

283. **ejaculate** *v.* (*n.* ejaculation, *n.* ejaculatory)—to utter suddenly, emotionally, and loudly. *Syn. v.* exclaim, declaim. *Ant. v.* mutter, murmur.

284. **eke** *v.*—to supplement; to make a living in a scanty fashion or bit by bit.

285. **elate** *v.* (*adj.* elated; *n.* elation)—to fill with joy or high spirits. *Syn. v.* exhilarate, enrapture (rapture), transport; *n.* jubilation; *adj.* exultant, rejoicing. *Ant. v.* dispirit; dishearten; *adj.* crestfallen; forlorn.

286. **elfish** *adj.* (*n.* elf, *adj.* elfin)—mischievous (in the nature of an elf). *Syn. adj.* prankish; weird; sprightly.

287. **elicit** *v.*—to draw forth or produce. *Syn. v.* evoke, educe.

288. **elite** *n.* (*n.*, *adj.* elitist, *n.* elitism)—a select or superior group enjoying special privileges. *Syn. adj.* eclectic, choice. *Ant. n.* rabble; *hoi polloi* (the common people).

289. **elude** *v.* (*adj.* elusive)—to evade. *Syn. adj.* evasive.

290. **emanate** *v.* (*n.* emanation)—to emit or issue forth. *Syn. v.* originate, exude, radiate.

291. **embezzle** *v.* (*n.* embezzlement, *n.* embezzler)—to steal or misuse entrusted funds. *Syn. v.* peculate, purloin, pilfer, filch, defalcate.

292. **eminent** *adj.* (*n.* eminence)—well-known; distinguished. *Syn. adj.* prominent, preeminent, reputable, illustrious; *n.* luminary; fame, glory. *Ant. adj.* disreputable, notorious (well-known in a bad sense).

293. **emissary** *n.*—an agent or representative messenger. *Syn. n.* herald, courier.

294. **emolument** *n.*—compensation; profit. *Syn. n.* remuneration (*adj.* remunerative), stipend.

295. **empathy** *n.* (*v.* empathize, *adj.* empathic—emotional sympathy for or appreciation and understanding of. *Syn. n.* identification, sympathy. *Ant. n.* apathy.

296. **empirical** *adj.* (*n.* empiricism)—guided by or based on experience, experiment or observation. *Ant. adj.* theoretical.

297. **emulate** *v.* (*n.* emulation, *adj.* emulous)—to strive to equal or excel through imitation. *Syn. v.* vie, rival.

298. **encumber** *v.* (*n.* encumbrance)—to weigh down; hinder. *Syn. v.* impede, clutter, hamper, burden, overload. (**cumbrous** *adj.*—weighty, bulky.) (**cumbersome** *n.*—burdensome.)

299. **endemic** *adj.*—restricted to, or prevalent in, a certain region. *Syn. adj.* indigenous, native.

300. **enigmatic** *adj.* (*n.* enigma)—puzzling. *Syn. adj.* inexplicable, perplexing, confusing.

301. **enjoin** *v.* (*n.* injunction)—to prohibit legally; to direct or impose authority. *Syn. v.* interdict, inhibit (restrain); command.

302. **ensue** *v.*—to follow as a result. *Syn. adj.* subsequent.

303. **enthrall** *v.*—to charm or captivate; to enslave. *Syn. v.* captivate, fascinate, thrill; spellbind.

304. **entice** *v.* (*adj.* enticing, *n.* enticement)—to lure by exciting hope or desire by subtle means, including flattery and guile. *Syn v.* allure, bait, cajole, inveigle, beguile (see **wheedle**), snare, decoy. *Ant. v.* deter, repel.

305. **entreat** *v.* (*n.* entreaty)—to plead with; to beg. *Syn. v.* supplicate (supplication, suppliant), importune, implore, beseech, solicit.

306. **envisage** *v.*—to visualize as a future possibility. *Syn. v.* envision.

307. **epicurean** *adj., n.* —disposed to pursue pleasurable or luxurious things in life. *Syn. adj., n.* hedonist *(n.* hedonism). *Ant. adj., n.* stoic *(n.* stoicism). **epicure** *n.* – one who cultivates fine taste in food; one with sensitive and discriminating tastes.

308. **epilogue** *n.* —a concluding section of a speech, literary work; a final issue of an action. *Ant. n.* prelude, prologue, preliminary, foreword, preface.

309. **epitaph** *n.* —a tombstone or monument inscription.

310. **epithet** *n.* —a word or phrase descriptive of a person's nature or position—(commonly *pejorative*).

311. **equivalent** *adj.* (*n.* equivalency)—tantamount (amounting, or practically equal, to). *Syn. adj.* identical.

312. **equivocate** *v.* (*n.* equivocation)—to use ambiguity deliberately to evade facing a main issue. *Syn. v.* quibble; double-talk. (**equivocal** *adj.* —intentionally having two possible meanings.)

313. **erode** *v.* (*n.* erosion)—to wear away. *Syn. v.* corrode.

314. **err** *v.* (*adj.* errant)—to make a mistake; to go astray. **erratic** *adj.* —straying, or deviating, from conventional conduct; eccentric. **erratum** *n.* (plural, *errata*)—a misprint. **erroneous** *adj.* —fallacious, mistaken.

315. **ersatz** *n.* —an inferior substitute. *Syn. adj.* synthetic; artificial.

316. **erstwhile** *adv.* —formerly; of old.

317. **erudite** *adj.* (*n.* erudition)—scholarly; profoundly learned. *Syn. n.* savant.

318. **escalate** *v.* (*n.* escalation)—to intensify or to increase gradually. *Syn. v.* accelerate, enlarge, widen. *Ant. v.* de-escalate; curtail.

319. **espionage** *n.* (*v.* espy)—spying. *Syn. n.* surveillance (close observation of a suspect), intelligence gathering.

320. **essay** *v.* —to try; to attempt. *Syn. v.* endeavor.

321. **establishment** *n.* —a group in power, controlling a particular activity or society.

322. **ethnic** *adj.* —pertaining to a racial or otherwise cultural society or system. **ethnology** *n.* (*adj.* ethnological)—the study of the elements of mankind (such as the races, their origins, distribution, and relations) involved in cultural growth. **ethical** *adj.* (*n.* ethics)—consistent with conventional regard for right and wrong. *Ant. adj.* unethical; immoral. **ethics** *n.* —moral principles. **ethic** *n.* —a body of values esteemed by a particular cultural group.

323. **etymology** *n.* (*adj.* etymological)—the science of the origin of words.

324. **eugenics** *n.* —the science concerned with improvement of mankind.

325. **euphoria** *n.* (*adj.* euphoric)—a state of well being.

326. **evince** *v.*—to show clearly; to provoke; to reveal. *Syn. v.* manifest, display, demonstrate.

327. **ewe** *n.*—a full-grown female sheep.

328. **exacerbate** *v.* (*n.* exacerbation)—to increase in bitterness or severity. *Syn. v.* embitter, aggravate, intensify. *Ant. v.* ameliorate, mollify, mitigate.

329. **excruciating** *adj.* (*n.* excruciation)—severely painful; causing anguish. *Syn. adj.* agonizing; extreme.

330. **exemplary** *adj.*—commendable; meriting imitation as a model. **exemplar** *n.*—an ideal or model person; a paragon (a model of excellence). **exemplify** *v.*—to illustrate or to serve as a pattern.

331. **exhort** *v.* (*n.* exhortation)—to warn; to urge or advise emphatically. *Syn. v.* admonish, importune, caution.

332. **exodus** *n.*—emigration (usually in large numbers). *Syn. n.* hegira: *Ant. n.* influx, incursion.

333. **exorcist** *n.* (*v.* exorcize, *n.* exorcism)—one capable of expelling an evil spirit.

334. **expedient** *n.* and *adj.* (*n.* expediency)—conveniently advantageous. *Syn. adj.* opportune (*n.* opportunist—one who takes unprincipled, self-seeking advantage of events or any means to achieve one's end), seasonable, politic. *Ant.* inexpedient, impolitic, untimely, inopportune.

335. **expedite** *v.* (*adj.* expeditious)—to speed up. *Syn. v.* dispatch, accelerate, facilitate; *adj.* fleeting (moving fast and lightly); transitory. *Ant. v.* retard, slacken; evanescent (vanishing by degrees).

336. **expound** *v.* (*n.* exposition, *adj.* expository, *n.* exponent)—to advocate or give a detailed explanation. *Syn. v.* expatiate, elucidate.

337. **extort** *v.* (*n.* extortion, *n.* extortionist)—to secure something by undue force or persuasion. *Syn. v.* wring, demand exactingly.

338. **extradite** *v.* (*n.* extradition)—to obtain for trial the surrender of a fugitive or prisoner from another's authority or jurisdiction.

339. **extrasensory** *adj.*—perceptible only by supernatural or other similar means.

340. **extrinsic** *adj.*—irrelevant; superfluous. *Syn. adj.* external; extraneous. *Ant. adj.* relevant, intrinsic (basic), inherent, innate.

341. **extrovert** *n.* (*n.* extroversion)—an outgoing person, concerned only with external matters rather than with the inner self. *Ant. n.* introvert (*n.* introversion).

342. **FACADE** *n.*—the front of a building; any front or outer appearance, frequently false or artificial. *Syn. n.* aspect.

343. **facet** *n.*—aspect, phase.

344. **facetious** *adj.* (*n.* facetiousness)—playfully humorous. *Syn. adj.* flippant, witty; *n.* levity. *Ant. adj.* grave, solemn, humorless.

345. **facile** *adj.* (*v.* facilitate, *n.* facility)—fluent; effortless.

346. **fad** *n.* (*adj.* faddish)—a popular fashion or craze, inclined to be passing.

347. **fallible** *adj.* (*n.* fallibility, *n.* fallacy)—likely to err or to be inaccurate. *Syn. adj.* fallacious (erring in logic), erroneous. *Ant. adj.* infallible, unmistakable.

348. **falter** *v.*—to stumble; to waver or hesitate in speech or action.

349. **fanatical** *adj.* (*n.* fanaticism)—extravagantly zealous or prejudiced. *Syn. adj.* perfervid, bigoted; *n.* extremist, zealot.

350. **fantastic** *adj.* (*n.* fantasy, *n.* fancy)—imaginary; unreal; queer. *Syn. adj.* fabulous, wondrous, remarkable, incredible, bizarre.

351. **fascism** *n.* (*adj.* fascistic)—a political system characterized by complete governmental dictatorship and control over industry, commerce, and political thinking.

352. **fastidious** *adj.* (*n.* fastidiousness)—demanding to a fault; fussy over precision; scornfully aloof. *Syn. adj.* finical, particular, meticulous; hypercritical, punctilious, squeamish, overnice; haughty, supercilious. *Ant. adj.* perfunctory.

353. **fealty** *n.*—loyalty; allegiance; faithfulness. *Syn. n.* fidelity, trust. *Ant. n.* treachery, betrayal, unfaithfulness.

354. **feasible** *adj.* (*n.* feasibility)—functionable; practicable. *Ant. adj.* unfeasible, impracticable, theoretical, academic.

355. **feat** *n.*—an extraordinary achievement, showing skill, boldness, or ingenuity. *Syn. n.* exploit.

356. **feckless** *adj.*—lacking in strength or firmness of spirit; worthless. *Syn. adj.* ineffective, feeble, shiftless.

357. **fecund** *adj.* (*n.* fecundity)—highly productive. *Syn. adj.* prolific, fruitful, lush. *Ant. adj.* unprolific, barren; arid.

358. **feign** *v.* (*n.* feint)—to pretend. *Syn. v.* simulate, dissemble, dissimulate.

359. **feline** *adj.*—characteristic of a cat; hence, sly, stealthy.

360. **felon** *n.*—a criminal. **felony** *n.* (*adj.* felonious)—a major crime.

361. **feminist** *n.* (*n.* feminism)—one who espouses equal rights for women.

362. **ferment** *n.*—a state of agitation or unrest. *Syn. n.* turbulence, row, commotion, excitement. *Ant. n.* tranquility.

363. **festoon** *v.*—to adorn with garlands (wreaths or circlets of flowers).

364. **fetish** *n.* (*n.* fetishism)—an object of blind devotion or worship. *Syn. n.* talisman, charm, amulet.

365. **fetter** *n.*—a chain that restrains movement. *Syn. n.* shackle: (figurative) restriction.

366. **fictitious** *adj.*—creatively imaginative; imaginary; nonexistent.

367. **fiery** *adj.* —intensely ardent; emotionally excitable; easily angered. *Syn. adj.* vehement, fervent, impassioned. *Ant. adj.* phlegmatic, lethargic, saturnine.

368. **filial** *adj.* —pertaining to a son or daughter.

369. **filly** *n.* —a young female horse; a mare.

370. **finesse** *n.* —delicacy of execution; adroitness. *Syn. n.* artfulness, skill, subtlety, craftiness (in a good or a bad sense).

371. **fiscal** *adj.* —pertaining to public or general personal finances. *Syn. adj.* monetary.

372. **flaccid** *adj.* —not firm; flabby. *Syn. adj.* limp.

373. **flag** *v.* —to droop, slow down, or decline in energy or interest. *Syn. v.* slacken. *Ant. v.* unflagging, indefatigable, unremitting, inexhaustible.

374. **flagrant** *adj.* (*n.* flagrancy)—shocking; grossly offensive. *Syn. adj.* outrageous, infamous, odious, scandalous, appalling.

375. **flair** *n.* —a natural talent; strong inclination. *Syn. n.* knack, bent. *Ant. n.* ineptitude, aversion.

376. **flaunt** *v.* —to show off. *Syn. v.* flourish, display (boldly or ostentatiously).

377. **flay** *v.* —to criticize sharply. *Syn. v.* excoriate, scathe.

378. **florid** *adj.* —ruddy; high-complexioned; exceedingly ornate. *Syn. adj.* rubicund; showy, decorative. *Ant. adj.* pallid (*n.* pallor), sallow, ashen, pale; simple, unadorned.

379. **flotsam** *n.* —floating cargo or wreckage of a sunken ship; discarded, useless odds and ends. *cf. n.* **jetsam** (cargo thrown off an overladen ship).

380. **flout** *v.* —to show or treat with contempt. *Syn. v.* mock, scorn, disdain, scoff at, gibe. *Ant. v.* conform, obey, respect.

381. **fluster** *v.* —to upset or confuse. *Syn. v.* bewilder, perturb, disconcert.

382. **foible** *n.* —a peculiarity or amusing weak point in a person. *Syn n.* peccadillo, eccentricity, imperfection.

383. **follower** *n.* —an adherent; a subordinate. *Syn. n.* disciple, apostle, partisan.

384. **folly** *n.* —a foolish or absurd action.

385. **forensic** *adj.* —relating to a public discussion or debate.

386. **forerunner** *n.* —someone going or sent in advance; a forecast. *Syn. n.* precursor, predecessor, herald, harbinger; omen, portent; ancestor.

387. **formidable** *adj.* —difficult to defeat; tending to arouse fear in a combat. *Syn. adj.* dreadful, redoubtable, awe-inspiring.

388. **forte** *n.* —a strong excelling point in someone.

389. **fortitude** *n.* —perseverance or courage in the face of adverse conditions. *Syn. n.* tenacity, stoicism, mettle, stamina.

390. **foster** *v.* —to nourish; to promote development or growth; to encourage. *Syn. v.* engender, nurture, cultivate. *Ant. v.* discourage, block.

391. **fracas** *n.* —a boisterous quarrel. *Syn. n.* brawl, uproar, fray.

392. **frenzy** *n.* (*adj.* frenzied)—hysterical mental agitation or enthusiasm. *Syn. n.* delirium (*adj.* delirious), madness, hysteria.

393. **frill** *n.* (*adj.* frilly)—useless, excessive elaborateness or ornamentation. *Syn. n.* frippery, finery.

394. **frivolous** *adj.* (*n.* frivolity)—light-minded; lacking in seriousness or importance. *Syn. adj.* trivial; silly; puerile. *Ant. adj.* serious, weighty, significant.

395. **frugal** *adj.* (*n.* frugality)—sparing or not wasteful in unnecessary expenditure; thrifty; economical. *Syn. adj.* stinting, skimping; parsimonious (excessive frugality), meager. *Ant. adj.* extravagant, spendthrift, prodigal.

396. **GAINFUL** *adj.*—profitable, yielding an income. *Syn. adj.* lucrative, remunerative.

397. **gala** *adj.*—festive.

398. **galvanize** *v.* (*adj.* galvanic)—to stimulate to sudden action; to electrify. *Syn. v.* spur on, arouse, excite.

399. **gamut** *n.*—a whole range or extent; scope. *Syn. n.* spectrum.

400. **garish** *adj.* (*n.* garishness)—excessively or tastelessly showy; ornate. *Syn. adj.* gaudy, tawdry (vulgarly decorative), flashy, glaring. *Ant. adj.* sober, modest.

401. **garrulous** *adj.* (*n.* garrulity)—customarily talkative. *Syn. adj.* loquacious, verbose, prolix, diffuse, wordy, voluble. *Ant. adj.* laconic, reticent.

402. **genealogy** *n.* (*adj.* genealogical)—a record or account of family history. *Syn. n.* lineage, pedigree.

403. **generous** *adj.* (*n.* generosity)—liberal or unselfish in giving assistance or sharing. *Syn. adj.* munificent, lavish, liberal, magnanimous, bountiful; high-minded. *Ant. adj.* selfish, miserly, stingy, stinting, meager, base, mean.

404. **genetics** *n.* (*adj.* genetic)—the branch of biology dealing with heredity.

405. **genre** *n.*—an art form or class. *Syn. n.* genus.

406. **genteel** *adj.*—pertaining to polite society; pretentiously refined. *Syn. adj.* well-bred, elegant, refined, affected.

407. **geriatrics** *n.*—the medical science dealing with the care of aged persons. *Syn. n.* gerontology. *Ant. n.* pediatrics (*n.* pediatrician).

408. **germane** *adj.*—closely related. *Syn. adj.* relevant, pertinent, fitting, apposite. *Ant. adj.* irrelevant. (**relate to** (vogue term)—having a sympathetic understanding of.)

409. **gesticulate** *v.* (*n.* gesticulation)—to make animated or expressive gestures of the body.

410. **ghastly** *adj.* (*n.* ghastliness)—horrible; deathlike. *Syn. adj.* frightful, grim, gruesome, macabre, grisly, shocking, forbidding, horrific, cadaverous.

411. **ghetto** *n.*—historically, a section of a city populated by a preponderance of Jews; a section of the city where members of a

minority racial or cultural group live. *Syn. n.* slum (vogue usage).

412. **gibberish** *n.* (*v.* gibber) – silly, trivial, commonly unintelligible talk. *Syn. n.* prattle

413. **glamor** *n.* (*adj.* glamorous, *v.* glamorize)—charm; good looks; a personal magical quality which excites admiration. *Syn. n.* charisma (*adj.* charismatic); enchantment, fascination.

414. **glean** *v.* —to gather patiently and with great effort.

415. **glib** *adj.* (*n.* glibness)—characterized by facile or commonly insincere speech. *Syn. adj.* fluent, smooth, slick.

416. **glitter** *v.* (*adj.* glittery)—to shine brightly; to sparkle. *Syn. v.* scintillate, gleam, glint, glisten; *adj.* brilliant, fulgent, luminous, effulgent, incandescent, lustrous, glossy; *n.* gloss. (*v.* gloss—to smooth over to make something deceptively attractive or acceptable; to give a misleading interpretation.) *Ant. adj.* murky, tenebrous, somber.

417. **glorify** *v.* (*n.* glorification)—to bestow glory, praise or honor upon a person or thing. *Syn. v.* glamorize, extol, adulate, exalt. *Ant. v.* denigrate, degrade, derogate.

418. **glower** *v.* —to frown; to stare at disapprovingly or angrily. *Syn. v.* glare, scowl.

419. **glutton** *n.* (*v.* glut)—one who eats or drinks to excess or overindulges in something. *Syn. n.* epicure, gourmand; *v.* gorge; *adj.* voracious, inordinate. *Ant. adj.* ascetic, abstemious, self-denying. (**gourmet** *n.* —one who has a cultivated taste in eating or drinking. *Syn. n.* epicure.)

420. **gossamery** *adj.* (*n.* gossamer)—fine, weblike or flimsy.

421. **gratify** *v.* (*n.* gratification)—to satisfy; to delight; to indulge or humor (one's feeling).

422. **gratis** *adv.* —without payment. *Syn. adj.* gratuitous. (**gratuity** *n.* —a tip.)

423. **gregarious** *adj.* —living with, or fond of, people in general. *Syn. adj.* sociable. *Ant. adj.* reclusive (*n.* recluse).

424. **grievous** *adj.* —intense; causing grief or pain. *Syn. adj.* flagrant, outrageous, atrocious, sorrowful, deplorable, heinous, grave. (**grievance** *n.* —complaint or cause for protest.)

425. **grimace** *n.* —a facial expression denoting an emotion, commonly one of disapproval or disgust.

426. **grime** *n.* (*adj.* grimy)—ingrained surface dirt. *Syn. v.* begrime, smudge; *n.* soot.

427. **gross** *adj.* (*n.* grossness)—extreme; vulgar; unrefined; wicked; immoral. *Syn. adj.* flagrant, coarse, indecent.

428. **grovel** *v.* —to abase oneself in anxiety to please. *Syn. v.* demean, ingratiate, fawn, truckle. *Ant. adj.* arrogant, overbearing.

429. **grueling** *adj.* —trying to the point of debilitation or exhaustion. *Syn. adj.* enervating, distressing, taxing (one's strength), exhausting. *Ant. n.* sinecure (effortless task or chore).

430. **guffaw** *n.*—a vulgar burst of hearty laughter.
431. **guile** *n.* (*adj.* guileful)—insidious craftiness. *Syn. n.* cunning, deceptiveness, duplicity, trickery, deceptive fraud; *adj.* wily. *Ant. adj.* guileless (free from guile), candid, artless, ingenuous, sincere.
432. **guilt** *n.*—wrongdoing. *Syn. n.* culpability, remorse (for a guilt committed), criminality. *Ant. n.* innocence; *adj.* innocuous.
433. **guise** *n.*—external appearance or form; deceptive appearance. *Syn. n.* pretense, semblance, aspect, garb.
434. **guru** *n.*—(literally) a spiritual leader, commonly a Hindu who inspires worship and absolute adherence; (figuratively) a charismatic leader or teacher with a worshipful following.
435. **gusto** *n.*—zestful enjoyment or relish.
436. **HALLMARK** *n.*—a mark or stamp betokening a standard of good quality or authenticity.
437. **harangue** *n.* and *v.*—a loud, vehement verbal attack before a public audience. *Syn. n.* rant, tirade; *adj.* rabble-rousing.
438. **harass** *v.* (*n.* harassment)— persistently to annoy or to badger. *Syn. v.* molest, hound, vex, nag.
439. **hardy** *adj.* (*n.* hardiness, *n.* hardihood)—(a) capable of withstanding hardship or fatigue; (b) courageous, stouthearted; (c) bold, foolhardy. *Syn.* (a) *adj.* sturdy, rugged, vigorous, robust, hale, stalwart. *Syn.* (b) *adj.* valiant, intrepid. *Ant.* (b) *adj.* craven, timorous. *Syn.* (c) *adj.* audacious, brazen, presumptuous.
440. **harrowing** *adj.* (*v.* harrow)—painfully distressing; inflicting torment. *Syn. adj.* vexatious, perturbing, tormenting, harrying.
441. **headlong** *adj.*—rash; impetuous. *Syn. adj.* reckless, incautious, hasty. *Ant. adj.* circumspect, wary.
442. **headstrong** *adj.*—determined to have one's own will. *Syn. adj.* stubborn, obdurate, obstinate. *Ant. adj.* docile, conciliatory, amenable, complaisant, tractable.
443. **heedless** *adj.* (*v.* heed)—inattentive; unmindful. *Syn. adj.* reckless, unwitting. *Ant. adj.* heedful, mindful.
444. **heifer** *n.*—a young cow.
445. **herculean** *adj.*—of extraordinary size or strength; exacting prodigious labor.
446. **heterodox** *adj.* (*n.* heterodoxy)—deviating from accepted beliefs or (church) doctrine. *Syn. n.* heretic (*adj.* heretical), iconoclasm (extreme heterodoxy). *Ant. adj.* orthodox, conventional, *n.* conformist.
447. **hierarchy** *n.* (*adj.* hierarchical)—a body of officials arranged in successive ranks of importance or authority; rule by ecclesiastics.
448. **histrionic** *adj.* (*n.* histrionics, *adj.* histrionical)—theatrical. *Syn. adj.* stagy, affected, overacting or overemotional.

449. **hoax** *n.*, *v.*—a practical joke; public deception or a fraudulent story.

450. **homily** *n.* (*adj.* homiletic)—a sermon.

451. **hoot** *v.*—to shout loudly, disapprovingly and contemptuously. *Syn. v.* jeer, deride (derisive), mock, gibe.

452. **hovel** *n.*—dirty, wretched living-quarters.

453. **hue** *n.* (a) shade or color; (b) a loud outcry; (c) aspect. *Syn* (a) *n.* tint.

454. **humanist** *n.* (*n.* humanism)—a person strongly concerned with human affairs; a scholar versed in the humanities. *Syn. n.* humanitarian.

455. **humdrum** *adj.*—monotonously dull. *Syn. adj.* prosaic, boring.

456. **hybrid** *adj.*—of mixed character or origin. *Syn. n.* crossbreed, mongrel; *adj.* heterogeneous.

457. **hyperbole** *n.* (*adj.* hyperbolic)—a figure of speech which is a deliberate overstatement. *Ant. n.* understatement.

458. **hypercritical** *adj.*—excessive, meticulous and petty faultfinding. *Syn. adj.* carping, caviling, captious.

459. **hypochondriac** *n.* (*adj.* hypochondriacal, *n.* hypochondria)—a person who is abnormally depressed over, and frequently tells about, his ailments which are often imaginary.

460. **hypocrisy** *n.* (*adj.* hypocritical, *n.* hypocrite) – the act of pretending to have virtues, feeling, or beliefs one knows one does not possess; hence, intentional insincerity.

461. **hypothesis** *n.* (*v.* hypothesize, *adj.* hypothetical)—a proposition tentatively assumed or posed, without sufficient evidence, to explain certain facts or to guide investigation. *Syn. n.* assumption, conjecture, premise.

462. **ICHTHYOLOGY** *n.*—a branch of zoology concerned with fish.

463. **idealist** *n.* (*adj.* idealistic, *v.* idealize, *n.* idealism)—a person holding high or noble standards and objectives, who envisions things in an ideal form rather than as they really are. *Syn. adj.* visionary, utopian, chimerical. *Ant. n.* pragmatist, realist, materialist.

464. **identify** *v.* (*n.* identity)—to associate oneself with, or recognize oneself as part of, a group.

465. **idiosyncrasy** *n.* (*adj.* idiosyncratic)—a personal peculiarity. *Syn. n.* quirk, crotchet (odd notion), vagary, eccentricity.

466. **idyllic** *adj.*—possessing the natural simplicity and charm commonly identified with rural scenery.

467. **ignominy** *n.* (*adj.* ignominious)—public disgrace. *Syn. n.* dishonor, infamy, obloquy, opprobrium, odium; *adj.* ignoble, discreditable, mean, despicable.

468. **illicit** *adj.*—illegal, unlawful.

469. **image** *n.*—a representation; an object of worship.

470. **imbroglio** *n.* (*v.* imbroil)—an entanglement or hostility resulting from a complicated misleading situation.

471. **imbue** *v.* —to penetrate deeply; to inspire. *Syn. v.* saturate, permeate, infuse, inspirit.

472. **immaculate** *adj.* (*n.* immaculateness)—spotless; pure; without blemish. *Syn. adj.* undefiled, flawless, impeccable (faultless, irreproachable).

473. **immolate** *v.* (*n.* immolation)—to sacrifice.

474. **immune** *adj.* (*n.* immunity, *v.* immunize, *n.* immunization)—free from penalty, obligation, infection. *Syn. adj.* exempt, unsusceptible; *n.* impunity. *Ant. adj.* liable.

475. **immutable** *adj.* (*n.* immutability)—unchangeable. *Syn. adj.* unalterable. *Ant. adj.* mutable.

476. **impact** *n.*, *v.* (*adj.* impacted)—the striking of one body against another; to pack closely. *Syn. v.* impinge, encroach, infringe, collide.

477. **impale** *v.* —to pierce with a sharp instrument. *Syn. v.* pierce, transfix, puncture.

478. **impeach** *v.* (*adj.* impeachable; *n.* impeachment)—to charge a public official with an offense in office. *Syn. v.* arraign (charge formally or at law), discredit, accuse, indict, incriminate (*adj.* incriminating). (**indict** *v.* (*n.* indictment, *adj.* indictable)—to charge formally with a crime or offense.)

479. **impend** *v.* (*adj.* impending)—to threaten to occur soon. *Syn. adj.* imminent, menacing.

480. **imperialism** *n.* (*adj.* imperialistic, *n.* imperialist)— a national policy of extending economic and political control over other dependent nations. *Syn. n.* hegemony.

481. **impervious** *adj.* —incapable of being penetrated or affected. *Syn. adj.* impermeable, impenetrable. *Ant. adj.* pervious, permeable.

482. **imponderable** *adj.* —incapable of being accurately measured, judged or weighed. *Ant. adj.* ponderable.

483. **impose** *v.* (*n.* imposition)—to foist upon; to intrude (*n.* intrusion). (**imposing** *adj.* —impressive.)

484. **impregnable** *adj.* —unconquerable. *Syn. adj.* indomitable, insuperable, unassailable, insurmountable, invincible, invulnerable. *Ant. adj.* surmountable, vincible, vulnerable.

485. **improvident** *adj.* (*n.* improvidence)—failing to make provision for future needs. *Syn. adj.* imprudent, incautious, shiftless, wasteful. *Ant. adj.* providential, prudent, thrifty.

486. **impudent** *adj.* (*n.* impudence)—rude; disrespectful. *Syn. adj.* insolent, pert; *n.* impertinence, effrontery, brazenness. *Ant. adj.* civil, affable.

487. **impugn** *v.* —to attack or challenge as false; to call into question. *Syn. v.* censure, make insinuations against.

488. **impute** *v.* —to attribute something (usually discreditable) to someone. *Syn. v.* ascribe. (**imputation** *n.* —accusation.)

489. **inception** *n.* (*adj.* incipient)—beginning. *Syn. n.* genesis, outset. *Ant. adj.* terminal; *n.* terminus.

490. **incessant** *adj.* —continuous without letup or remission. *Syn. adj.* continuous, constant, chronic, ceaseless, unceasing, perpetual, relentless. *Ant. adj.* recurrent, intermittent, infrequent, sporadic; *n.* respite.

491. **incognito** *adj., adv.* —with one's identity concealed.

492. **incontrovertible** *adj.* —uncontestable or indisputable. *Syn. adj.* irrefutable, indubitable, undeniable. *Ant. adj.* moot (debatable).

493. **incorporeal** *adj.* —without body or substance. *Syn. adj.* spiritual, intangible; unsubstantial. *Ant. adj.* corporeal, tangible, materialistic.

494. **incubus** *n.* —an oppressive or burdensome (like a nightmare) weight.

495. **incumbent** *adj.* (*n.* incumbency)—currently holding office; obligatory.

496. **indemnity** *n.* (*v.* indemnify)—compensation for damage or loss; protection against future loss. *Syn. n.* reparation, amends, expiation, redress, restitution.

497. **indoctrinate** *v.* (*v.* indoctrinize, *n.* indoctrination)—to brainwash or propagandize by persistent instruction in a doctrine or major system of beliefs. *Syn. v.* inculcate; imbue.

498. **ineffable** *adj.* —incapable of being expressed. *Syn. adj.* inexpressible, unspeakable, indescribable.

499. **infatuation** *n.* —extravagant or foolish love or devotion. **infatuate** *v.* —to inspire with a foolish passion. *Syn. n.* doting.

500. **infer** *v.* (*n.* inference)—to conclude from an implicit statement or data. *Syn. v.* deduce (*n.* deduction).

501. **infidel** *n.* —an unbeliever. (**infidelity** *n.* —disloyalty, unfaithfulness.)

502. **inflate** *v.* (*n.* inflation, *adj.* inflationary)—to swell; to expand abnormally; to increase unduly. (**inflated** *adj.* (language)—pompous, turgid.) *Ant. v.* deflate, attenuate (thin out); *n.* attrition (slow diminution, especially in strength or ability to endure).

503. **inflict** *v.* (*n.* infliction)—to assault or impose (punishment, aggression).

504. **infraction** *n.* —violation of a law or regulation. *Syn. n.* breach, infringement.

505. **ingratiate** *v.* (*n.* ingratiation)—to try to establish and win one's way into another's favor or good graces. (**ingratiating** *adj.* —charming.) *Syn. v.* fawn, insinuate; *adj.* sycophantic.

506. **iniquity** *n.* (*adj.* iniquitous)—gross injustice or wickedness; an immoral act. *Syn. n.* evil, moral turpitude, sinfulness; *adj.* nefarious. *Ant. n.* righteousness.

507. **innovate** *v.* (*n.* innovation *adj.* innovative) to introduce a new

creation. *Syn. v.* initiate.

508. **inordinate** *adj.* —excessive; immodest. *Syn. adj.* exorbitant. *Ant. adj.* reasonable.

509. **inquest** *n.* —a judicial investigation, especially into a person's death. (**inquisition** *n.* (*adj.* inquisitorial)—a severe official investigation.)

510. **insatiable** *adj.* (*adj.* insatiate)—incapable of being satisfied or appeased. *Syn. adj.* greedy, unappeasable. *Ant. adj.* satiable.

511. **inscrutable** *adj.* —mysterious,; defying human comprehension or scrutiny. *Syn. adj.* enigmatic, unfathomable, impenetrable, incomprehensible.

512. **insipid** *adj.* (*n.* insipidity)—tasteless; dull. *Syn. adj.* vapid, jejune, bland, unpalatable. *Ant. adj.* succulent, sapid, piquant, racy, stimulating.

513. **instigate** *v.* (*n.* instigation)—to provoke into action (pejorative). *Syn. v.* spur, incite, goad, foment, egg on.

514. **insurrection** *n.* —open uprising or resistance against established authority. *Syn. n.* rebellion, insurgency (*n.* insurgent), mutiny.

515. **integrate** *v.* (*n.* integration)—to unite into one whole. *Syn v.* unify, desegregate, consolidate, incorporate, amalgamate, meld. *Ant. v.* segregate, stratify. (**integral** *adj.* —basic, intact, essential.)

516. **integrity** *n.* —uprightness; moral honesty. *Syn. n.* rectitude, probity.

517. **intelligentsia** *n.* —the intellectual, highly cultivated rank within society. *Syn. n.* elite. *Ant. n.* masses, rabble, *hoi polloi*, proletariat.

518. **intervene** *v.* (*n.* intervention, *n.* and *adj.* interventionist)—to intercede; to interfere; to occur between points in time. *Syn. v.* interpose.

519. **intransigent** *adj.* —unyielding; uncompromising.

520. **inure** *v.* —to harden by long exposure or suffering. *Syn. v.* indurate.

521. **inveigh** *v.* (*adj.* invective)—violently to assail or denounce verbally. *Syn. v.* rail, vituperate, fulminate.

522. **invidious** *adj.* (*n.* invidiousness)—arousing ill will or giving offense. *Syn. adj.* resentful, hateful.

523. **irascible** *adj.* (*n.* irascibility)—readily angered or annoyed. *Syn. adj.* short-tempered, irritable, touchy, choleric. *Ant. adj.* even-tempered, equable.

524. **ire** *n.* (*adj.* irate)—anger; wrath; rage.

525. **iridescent** *adj.* (*n.* iridescence)—exhibiting rainbowlike colors.

526. **irksome** *adj.* —annoyingly tedious; tiresome or boring.

527. **irony** *n.* (*adj.* ironic)—(a) a mode of speech or writing in which the expressed meaning is the opposite of the literal meaning.

(b) an unexpected outcome of events which appears to mock the intended or expressed outcome.

528. **itinerant** *n.*, *adj.*—traveling from place to place. *Syn. adj.* peregrinating, migratory, peripatetic, nomadic (*n.* nomad). (**itinerary** *n.*—a journey plan or travel route.)

529. **JADED** *adj.*—overworked; worn out; dulled by dissipation.

530. **jargon** *n.*—specialized language of a particular trade; unintelligible speech. *Syn. n.* cant, gibberish, twaddle.

531. **jeopardize** *v.* (*n.* jeopardy)—to endanger. *Syn. v.* imperil, hazard.

532. **jostle** *v.*—to push or brush roughly against. *Syn. v.* shove, bump (against).

533. **juggernaut** *n.*—an irresistible overpowering crushing force.

534. **KLEPTOMANIA** *n.* (*n.* kleptomaniac)—an obsessive inclination to steal, especially without economic motive.

535. **knell** *n.*—(literally) the mournful sound by a bell announcing a death or funeral; (figuratively) any sound indicating the end or failure of something. *Syn. n.* and *v.* toll.

536. **knuckle** *v.*—to submit or yield to pressure.

537. **LACERATE** *v.* (*n.* laceration)—to inflict severe cuts and tears on a body; to distress mentally, emotionally, or physically. *Syn. v.* maim, wound, mangle, mutilate.

538. **lachrymose** *adj.* (*adj.* lachrymal)—tearful; habitually inclined to weeping and sentimental melancholy. *Syn. adj.* mournful.

539. **lackadaisical** *adj.*—lacking in vigor, enthusiasm, or determination. *Syn. adj.* listless, lethargic; *n.* lassitude. *Ant. adj.* dynamic, energetic, vivacious.

540. **lackey** *n.*—servile attendant or follower. *Syn. n.* cultist, disciple; toady, apple-polisher, jackal, flunky, minion, bootlicker, sycophant; *adj.* obsequious (humble, deferential), subservient; *v.* kowtow. (**satellite** *n.*—a country completely dominated by another.)

541. **laggard** *n.*, *adj.*—one who falls behind; lingering; loitering. *Syn. adj.* dilatory, sluggish, languid. *Ant. adj.* punctilious, meticulous, vibrant, vivacious.

542. **laissez faire** *n.*—a theory or policy espousing noninterference by government in trade or other economic affairs. *Syn. n.* free enterprise. *Ant. n.* totalitarianism; fascism.

543. **lament** *v.* (*n.* lamentation, *adj.* lamentable)—to bewail; to express sorrow for. *Syn. v.* mourn, grieve, moan, bemoan, wail, regret. *Ant. v.* rejoice, jubilate.

544. **larceny** *n.* (*adj.* larcenous)—theft.

545. **leer** *n.*—a sidelong glance, especially an insulting, licentious, suggestive, distrustful, or scornful look.

546. **lenient** *adj.* (*n.* leniency)—lax; mild. *Syn. adj.* permissive, indulgent, clement. *Ant. adj.* stringent, harsh, inclement, severe.

547. **lethal** *adj.* —deadly or fatal; decisively destructive. *Syn. adj.* mortal.
548. **lexicon** *n.* —dictionary.
549. **liaison** *n.* —a link between different groups; an intimate illicit relationship between a woman and a man. *Syn. n.* connection, affair.
550. **libel** *n. (adj.* libelous)—a defamatory, falsely written statement or reference, maliciously or unfairly injurious to a person's reputation. *Syn. n.* calumny, aspersion, misrepresentation, defamation.
551. **libido** *n. (adj.* libidinal)—the sexual instinct; sexual desire. (**libidinous** *adj.* —characteristic of the libido; lustful)
552. **limber** *adj.* —readily flexible. *Syn. adj.* supple, lithe, pliant, pliable. *Ant. adj.* inflexible, unbending, rigid.
553. **limpid** *adj. (n.* limpidity)—clear or transparent. *Syn. adj.* pellucid, intelligible.
554. **lineament** *n.* —a distinctive character, as of the face; a distinguishing feature.
555. **liquidate** *v. (n.* liquidation)—to pay off a debt; to end a business; to dispose of, as by killing or eradication (a political enemy).
556. **litany** *n.* —a ceremonious series of religious prayers and congregational responses; a long monotonous recital of accounts or complaints.
557. **literal** *adj. (n.* literalness)—explicit in meaning; representing exact translation; word for word (verbatim). *Ant. adj.* figurative, metaphorical; *n.* paraphrase.
558. **litigate** *v. (n.* litigation)—to go to law for adjudication of a dispute. **litigious** *adj.* —habitually resorting to lawsuits; argumentative, contentious.
559. **livid** *adj.* —ashen or deathly pale; black and blue from a bruise; the whitish color of one enraged.
560. **longevity** *n.* —long life.
561. **low** *v.* —to utter a sound characteristic of cattle. (**lower** *v.* —to scowl; to frown darkly; to threaten (as a darkening sky).)
562. **lubricate** *v. (n.* lubrication)—to oil or grease so as to make smooth and slippery.
563. **ludicrous** *adj.* —ridiculous. *Syn. adj.* laughable, risible, farcical, preposterous, absurd.
564. **lull** *n., v.* —to soothe or render quiet; to quiet down (a disorderly condition); a temporary condition of stillness.
565. **lurid** *adj. (n.* luridness)—shockingly vivid or sensational. *Syn. adj.* gruesome, revolting.
566. **lurk** *v.* —to lie concealed in waiting; to go about secretly. *Syn. v.* skulk.
567. **MACHIAVELLIAN** *adj.* —using craft or deceit to gain political superiority; unscrupulous. *Syn. adj.* cunning, subtle,

astute. *Ant. adj.* ingenuous, high-principled; *n.* integrity.

568. **magnificence** *n.* (*adj.* magnificent)—great beauty, luxury, or lavishness. *Syn. n.* grandeur, splendor; *adj.* grand, opulent, stately, superlatively sumptuous, majestic.

569. **maim** *v.*—to damage; to mutilate; to cripple or mangle. *Syn. v.* impair, deface, lacerate.

570. **malaise** *n.*—a feeling of general discomfort, uneasiness, or moral apathy.

571. **malfeasance** *n.*—illegal wrongdoing (especially by a public official). (**misfeasance** *n.*—improper conduct in public office.)

572. **malice** *n.* (*adj.* malicious)—spite; deep-seated ill will. *Syn. n.* rancor (*adj.* rancorous), venom, malevolence. *Ant. n.* good will; benevolence.

573. **mandate** *n., v.*—(a) an authorized demand to pursue a certain course of action; (b) the expressed will of voters directed toward their representatives; (c) to maintain a consigned trusteeship of a territory. *Syn. n.* injunction, consignment. **mandatory** *adj.*—authoritatively receiving a command or mandate; obligatory. *Syn. adj.* imperative. *Ant. adj.* optional, discretionary.

574. **maneuver** *n.*—a battle strategy or other contest; a clever or skillful move or manipulation. *Syn. n.* ruse, stratagem, tactics, strategy.

575. **manifest** *adj.*—clear; plain; readily perceived. *Syn. adj.* apparent, obvious, ostensible. *Ant. adj.* incomprehensible, inscrutable, enigmatic. (**manifesto** *n.*—a public declaration, proclamation, promulgation.)

576. **maritime** *adj.*—situated or residing near the sea; concerned with sea and shipping. *Syn. adj.* nautical, naval, marine. *Ant. adj.* terrestrial.

577. **martinet** *n.*—a stringent disciplinarian.

578. **masochism** *n.* (*n.* masochist)—a perverted pleasure in physical or mental suffering inflicted on one by oneself or by another.

579. **mastodon** *n.*—one of several extinct animals.

580. **maternal** *adj.* (*n.* maternity)—pertaining to motherhood. **paternal** *adj.* (*n.* paternity)—pertaining to fatherhood. (**paternalism** *n.*—benevolent colonialism.)

581. **matriculate** *v.* (*n.* matriculation)—to enroll at a college or university.

582. **maudlin** *adj.*—excessively or tearfully sentimental. *Syn. adj.* mawkish, effusive, lachrymal.

583. **maze** *n.*—a complex and confusing network. *Syn. n.* labyrinth.

584. **meander** *v.*—to wander idly without any set objective. *Syn. v.* ramble, rove, amble, roam, gad, gallivant, saunter.

585. **media** *n., pl.* (*sing.*, **medium**)—means of mass communication.

586. **megalomania** *n.* (*n.* megalomaniac)—obsessive delusion of great

personal importance or grandeur.

587. **megalopolis** *n.*—a region comprising several adjoining urban areas and centering around a metropolis.

588. **mellow** *adj.* (*n.* mellowness)—ripened and softened by time. *Ant. adj.* green, immature.

589. **memento** *n.*—something bringing forth a remembrance. *Syn. n.* keepsake, relic.

590. **mendacious** *adj.* (*n.* mendacity)—lying. *Syn. adj.* prevaricating, fabricating; *n.* untruth. *Ant. adj.* veracious (*n.* veracity).

591. **mendicant** *adj., n.* (*n.* mendicancy)—begging (for alms); a beggar.

592. **menial** *adj.*—servile; in the nature of a domestic servant. *Syn. adj.* degrading; *n.* hireling, attendant.

593. **meretricious** *adj.*—appearing only superficially attractive or impressive; showy; deceitfully ornamental. *Syn. adj.* specious, spurious.

594. **mesmerize** *v.* (*n.* mesmerism)—to hypnotize; to spellbind.

595. **metamorphosis** *n.* (*v.* metamorphose)—a complete transformation. *Syn. n.* transmutation, mutation. *Ant. adj.* immutable.

596. **meticulous** *adj.*—excessively exacting or scrupulous about details. *Syn. adj.* punctilious, finical, fastidious.

597. **mew** *n.*—a sound characteristic of a cat.

598. **microcosm** *n.*—a world or universe in miniature. *Ant. n.* macrocosm.

599. **milieu** *n.*—surroundings; environment; setting. *Syn. n.* ambience.

600. **millennium** *n.*—a period of 1000 years; figuratively, a period of unalloyed happiness.

601. **mimic** *n., adj., v.* (*n.* mimicry, *adj.* mimetic)—an imitator (often playful). *Syn. v.* mime (imitate through gestures, charade), simulate, ape, impersonate; *adj.* imitative.

602. **minuscule** *n.*—very small; minimal.

603. **misanthropic** *adj.* (*n.* misanthropy, *n.* misanthrope, *n.* misanthropist)—displaying hatred or distrust of mankind. *Ant. adj.* philanthropic, humanitarian, eleemosynary.

604. **misconstrue** *v.* (*n.* misconstruction)—to misinterpret another's sense or motives. *Syn. v.* misjudge.

605. **misdemeanor** *n.*—a criminal offense less grave than the major crime of felony.

606. **misgiving** *n.*—a feeling of hesitation, doubt, regret, apprehension, or uneasiness. *Syn. n.* qualm.

607. **misogyny** *n.* (*n.* misogynist)—hatred, fear or distrust of women.

608. **moderate** *v., adj.* (*n.* moderation)—to mediate; to arbitrate; not extreme or severe. *Syn. v.* ameliorate, calm, pacify; *adj.* temperate, mild, calm. *Ant. adj.* radical.

609. **modicum** *n.*—a small amount. *Syn. adj.* picayune, trifling, paltry; *n.* pittance. *Ant. adj.* copious; *n.* plethora, cornucopia.

610. **moratorium** *n.*—a period of, a legal authorization for, deferring

payment of debt; a delay officially required or granted.

611. **morbid** *adj.* (*n.* morbidity)—unwholesomely depressing or gruesome. *Syn. adj.* sickly, unhealthy.

612. **mores** *n.*—customs, traditions; customary moral attitudes.

613. **mote** *n.*—a small bit; a speck.

614. **motley** *adj.*—of various mixed colors, shapes, elements. *Syn. adj.* medley, variegated, heterogeneous.

615. **mulct** *v.*—to deprive of or obtain money by trickery, fraud or extortion.

616. **mundane** *adj.*—worldly; unspiritual. *Syn. adj.* temporal, secular, earthly.

617. **myopic** *adj.* (*n.* myopia)—near-sighted.

618. **myriad** *adj.*—innumerable. *Syn. adj.* multitudinous.

619. **mystique** *n.*—a mystical power in a person or a person's actions that attracts others. *Syn. n.* aura, charisma.

620. **NETTLE** *v.*—to irritate. *Syn. v.* vex, irk, provoke (*n.* provocation), pique. *Ant. v.* charm, disarm, beguile.

621. **neurosis** *n.* (*adj.* neurotic)—nervousness without organic cause, characterized by obsessions, phobias.

622. **noisome** *adj.*—foul smelling; disgustingly odorous. *Syn. adj.* fetid. *Ant. adj.* aromatic, fragrant.

623. **nominal** *adj.*—in name only or of token importance. *Syn. adj.* symbolic.

624. **nonchalant** *adj.* (*n.* nonchalance)—appearing casually indifferent. *Syn. adj.* detached, insouciant, lackadaisical.

625. **nonentity** *n.*—a person (or thing) of little or no importance; nonexistence.

626. **nostalgia** *n.* (*adj.* nostalgic)—homesickness. *Syn. n.* pining, sentimentality, longing.

627. **nostrum** *n.*—a quack medicine; a cure-all. *Syn. n.* panacea, a pet remedy.

628. **novice** *n.* (*n.* novitiate)—a beginner. *Syn. n.* newcomer, neophyte, tyro.

629. **numismatist** *n.*—a collector of coins.

630. **nuptial** *adj.*—pertaining to a marriage or wedding ceremony. *Syn. adj.* matrimonial, conjugal, connubial.

631. **OBITUARY** *n.*—a newspaper notice of a death, often joined with a brief biography of the deceased.

632. **objectionable** *adj.*—offensive; evoking disapproval. *Syn. adj.* disagreeable, insulting.

633. **oblivious** *adj.* (*n.* oblivion)—forgetful; unmindful. *Syn. adj.* inadvertent, unaware.

634. **obscene** *adj.* (*n.* obscenity)—indecent in language or action; immoral; loathsome; repulsive; disgusting; immodest. *Syn. adj.* pornographic, smutty, scatalogical, lewd, salacious, lascivious, licentious.

635. **obsession** *n.* (*adj.* obsessional, *adj.* obsessive)—an uncontrollable,

morbid preoccupation with a set feeling or idea. *Syn. n.* compulsion, phobia (*adj.* phobic—having morbid fear or aversion), craze, mania.

636. **obtrusive** *adj.* (*v.* obtrude, *n.* obtrusion)—pushy; aggressive; protruding. *Syn. adj.* brash, intrusive, protuberant (bulging, jutting out).

637. **occult** *adj.* (*n.* occultism)—relating to magic or the supernatural. *Syn. adj.* mysterious, inscrutable, supernatural, mystical, metaphysical.

638. **oligarchy** *n.* (*adj.* oligarchical)—control of government by a few persons or a powerful clique.

639. **ominous** *adj.* (*n.* omen)—foreshadowing evil. *Syn. adj.* portentous (*n.* portent), inauspicious, foreboding, sinister; *n.* premonition, presentiment.

640. **omnipotent** *adj.* (*n.* omnipotence)—all-powerful.

641. **omnipresent** *adj.*—existing or observable everywhere. *Syn. adj.* prevalent, ubiquitous.

642. **omniscient** *adj.* (*n.* omniscience)—knowing much or everything. *Syn. adj.* knowledgeable, well informed.

643. **omnivorous** *adj.*—having an insatiable, undiscriminating appetite for a variety of things, such as reading or food; eating everything, especially both animal and vegetable food.

644. **onus** *n.* (*adj.* onerous)—a burden; responsibility; blame.

645. **opt** *v.* (*n.* option, *adj.* optional)—to choose between two or more equally available offerings.

646. **optimum** *n.*—the most favorable degree, point or condition.

647. **orient** *v.* (*n.* orientation)—to familiarize with, or adjust to, a new situation or study.

648. **oscillate** *v.* (*n.* oscillation)—to waver between two courses. *Syn. v.* fluctuate, sway, vacillate; *adj.* indecisive, ambivalent (wavering between two coexistent contrary opinions or attitudes). *Ant. adj.* unwavering, inflexible.

649. **ostentation** *n.* (*adj.* ostentatious)—a boastful, lavish, or pretentious display. *Syn. adj.* pretentious, flashy, ornate, flamboyant. *Ant. adj.* unostentatious, plain, retiring.

650. **ostracize** *v.* (*n.* ostracism)—to exclude (someone) from society by general consent. *Syn. v.* banish, proscribe, exile; *n.* expatriation (forced or voluntary emigration or expulsion from one's country), pariah (social outcast).

651. **outwit** *v.*—to surpass by superior astuteness or craft.

652. **PALTRY** *adj.*—insignificant; trivial; of little worth. *Syn. adj.* petty, minor, slight, trifling, nugatory. *Ant. adj.* significant, momentous, major, critical.

653. **panorama** *n.* (*adj.* panoramic)—a continuous moving picture, slowly unfolding an extended representation of a landscape or other scene; a comprehensive coverage of a subject or a chain of events. *Syn. n.* kaleidoscope.

654. **parable** *n.*—a short, simple, often allegorical, narrative designed to convey a moral or religious lesson.

655. **paradox** *n.* (*adj.* paradoxical)—a seemingly self-contradictory statement, which may prove valid on closer examination.

656. **paramount** *adj.*—uppermost; supreme; superior in power. *Syn. adj.* foremost, preeminent, dominant.

657. **paranoia** *n.* (*adj.* paranoid)—a mental disorder characterized by delusions of being persecuted or of hostility by others.

658. **parody** *n.*—a comic imitation of the style and manner of a serious literary production. *Syn. n.* mimicry, burlesque, satire, lampoon.

659. **paroxysm** *n.*—a sudden vehement outburst of emotion or action. *Syn. n.* spasm.

660. **parvenu** *n.*—one who has recently risen to a higher position of wealth but lacks the suitable concomitant social qualifications. *Syn. n.* upstart.

661. **pathology** *n.* (*adj.* pathological)—a study of the nature and cause of a disorder or disease.

662. **pathos** *n.* (*adj.* pathetic)—a quality in a work of art or in an experience that arouses pity or sympathy.

663. **pedantic** *adj.* (*n.* pedant)—given to showing off one's bookish learning. (**pedagogue** *n.*—a school teacher, usually one who is dogmatic.) (**pedantry** *n.*—instruction characterized by prime concern for rules and details.)

664. **peerless** *adj.* (*n.* peer)—without an equal; unrivaled. *Syn. adj.* unmatched, unexcelled.

665. **peevish** *adj.* (*n.* peeve)—easily annoyed or upset; given to airing complaints. *Syn. adj.* crotchety, testy, splenetic, petulant, querulous, choleric. *Ant. adj.* complaisant, even-tempered.

666. **pejorative** *n.*, *adj.*—having a derogatory sense or force. *Syn. adj.* disparaging, denigrating, depreciative.

667. **penal** *adj.* (*v.* penalize, *n.* penalty)—pertaining to punishment. *Syn. adj.* punitive (**penitentiary** *n.*—prison.)

668. **penchant** *n.*—a decided inclination, tendency or taste for something. *Syn. n.* predilection, proclivity; *adj.* prone. *Ant. n.* disinclination, aversion.

669. **pensive** *adj.* (*n.* pensiveness)—wistfully, solemnly, or profoundly thoughtful. *Syn. adj.* contemplative, meditative, reflective. *Ant. adj.* nonchalant, carefree, lackadaisical.

670. **peregrinate** *v.* (*n.* peregrination)—to travel or wander from one place to another. *Syn. n.* pilgrimage. (**pilgrimage** *n.*—a journey to a sacred place.) (**pilgrim** *n.*—any traveler to a sacred place.)

671. **peremptory** *adj.*—final; decisive; dictatorial. *Syn. adj.* absolute, dogmatic, imperious.

672. **perfidious** *adj.* (*n.* perfidy)—breaching a trust; treacherous. *Syn. adj.* insidious, disloyal, unfaithful.

673. **persevere** *v.* (*adj.* persevering; *n.* perseverance)—to persist in the face of drawbacks. *Syn. adj.* pertinacious, tenacious. (**pertinacious** *adj.* (*n.* pertinacity)—dogged.) (**tenacious** *adj.* (*n.* tenacity)—steadfast.)

674. **perspicuous** *adj.* (*n.* perspicuity)—clear; easily comprehensible; lucidly expressed.

675. **perturbed** *adj.* (*n.* perturbation)—profoundly, inwardly upset. *Syn. adj.* disquieted, agitated, troubled.

676. **peruse** *v.* (*n.* perusal)—to read with care. *Syn. v.* scrutinize.

677. **pervade** *v.* (*adj.* pervasive)—to spread through. *Syn. v.* diffuse, infiltrate, saturate, permeate (*adj.* permeable).

678. **philatelist** *n.*—a stamp collector.

679. **pithy** *adj.*—pointed; concise; meaningful. *Syn. adj.* terse, sententious, cogent, succinct. *Ant. adj.* diffusive, prolix.

680. **plagiarism** *n.* (*n.* plagiary, *v.* plagiarize)—palming off another's writing as one's own or using such work without permission. *Syn. n.* piracy.

681. **plausible** *adj.* (*n.* plausibility)—apparently true, valid, or reasonable. *Syn. adj.* credible, specious. (**specious** *adj.*—a deceptive or false outward semblance of being true; superficially fair, just, or correct; meretricious.)

682. **plebeian** *adj.*—characteristic of the lower classes; hence, crude and vulgar.

683. **plight** *n.*, *v.*—an adverse or difficult situation; to give a pledge. *Syn. n.* a predicament, dilemma, quandary.

684. **ploy** *n.*—a tactic used to secure an advantage. *Syn. n.* gimmick, maneuver.

685. **plutocrat** *n.* (*n.* plutocracy, *adj.* plutocratic)—one who wields ruling power because he is wealthy.

686. **politicking** *n.*—political campaigning.

687. **pompous** *adj.* (*n.* pomposity, *n.* pomp)—making a pretentious show of position or importance; high-flown or inflated in language. *Syn. adj.* bombastic, ostentatious, (self-consciously) formal, lofty, stodgy, stuffy. *Ant. adj.* natural, simple.

688. **ponderous** *adj.* (*adj.* ponderable)—large and unwieldy; graceless in action. *Syn. adj.* massive, huge, weighty, hefty. (**ponder** *v.*—to deliberate; to ruminate; to reflect; to meditate.)

689. **potent** *adj.* (*n.* potency, *adj.* potential)—powerful; mighty; influential. *Syn. adj.* effective, convincing, cogent.

690. **potpourri** *n.*—a mixture of various incongruous elements. *Syn. n.* melange, conglomeration, heterogeneity, miscellany, medley, farrago.

691. **precarious** *adj.*—dangerously uncertain or unstable. *Syn. adj.* perilous, insecure, hazardous.

692. **precipitous** *adj.* (*n.* precipice)—(a) extremely steep; (b) rash and hasty in action. *Syn. adj.* headlong, impetuous, reckless.

Ant. adj. shallow.

693. **precocious** *adj.* (*n.* precocity, *n.* precociousness)—prematurely bright. *Ant. adj.* puerile (immature), retarded.

694. **predatory** *adj.* (*adj.* predacious)—plundering. *Syn. adj.* pillaging, preying, marauding, rapacious; *n.* pelf, loot.

695. **prerogative** *n.*—privilege assumed as an exclusive right coming either from heritage or from an office or rank held. *Syn. n.* **perquisite** (an advantage coming with one's position or office).

696. **prestigious** *adj.* (*n.* prestige)—highly reputed or esteemed. *Syn. adj.* reputable, estimable, renowned.

697. **presumptuous** *adj.* (*n.* presumption)—boldly impertinent or assuming. *Syn. adj.* audacious, arrogant.

698. **privy** (**to**) *adj.*—exclusively sharing in the knowledge of something private or secret.

699. **probe** *n.*, *v.*—to search out thoroughly; to investigate. *Syn. v.* explore, scrutinize.

700. **prognosticate** *v.* (*n.* prognostication)—to foretell. *Syn. v.* portend, forebode, presage, augur, adumbrate; *adj.* predictive. (**prognosis** *n.* (*n.* prognostic)—prediction of a probable future course.)

701. **proliferate** *v.* (*n.* proliferation, *adj.* proliferative)—to branch out or to increase in numbers, as by rapid reproduction of new parts. *Syn. v.* expand, swell, spread. *Ant. v.* narrow, contract, shrivel, shorten, reduce.

702. **prosaic** *adj.*—commonplace; dull; unimaginative. *Syn. adj.* vapid, cliche, matter-of-fact, humdrum, literal, stodgy.

703. **prospectus** *n.*—a preliminary statement of a new venture, as a business undertaking, a literary work, or a private school.

704. **proviso** *n.* (*n.* provision)—a condition for agreement or contract. *Syn. n.* stipulation, provision, restriction, qualification. *Ant. adj.* unqualified, unreserved.

705. **prowess** *n.*—outstanding bravery, skill, or strength.

706. **pseudo** *adj.*—false or counterfeit.

707. **pulchritude** *n.* (*adj.* pulchritudinous)—physical beauty. *Syn. n.* comeliness.

708. **puritanical** *adj.* (pejorative)—austere; rigid with respect to religious observance or moral standards. *Syn. adj.* prudish (excessive sexual modesty), stern; *n.* prudery.

709. **purport** *v.*, *n.*—to profess; intended meaning.

710. **purview** *n.*—the full scope or range of authority, vision, or comprehension.

711. **putrid** *adj.* (*adj.* putrified)—rotten; corrupt. *Syn. adj.* decaying, (offensively) odorous, fetid; depraved.

712. **pyromaniac** *n.* (*n.* pyromania)—a person obsessed with an uncontrollable impulse to set fires.

713. **QUELL** *v.*—to suppress forcibly (as a riot); to subdue. *Syn. v.*

crush, quench, quash; *v.* vanquish, pacify, compose, allay. *Ant. v.* foster, incite, instigate; *v.* excite, agitate, exacerbate.

714. **questionable** *adj.*—(a) open to doubt or dispute; (b) doubtful respectability, honesty, or morality. *Syn. adj.* problematic.

715. **quirk** *n.*—a personal eccentricity. *Syn. n.* vagary, whim, caprice.

716. **quixotic** *adj.*—idealistic in an impractical manner; extravagantly chivalrous. *Syn. adj.* fantastic, visionary, utopian. *Ant. n.* pragmatist, realist.

717. **quizzical** *adj.*—comical; odd; puzzling.

718. **RABID** *adj.*—violently fanatical; extreme in views. *Syn. adj.* raging, zealous, furious. *Ant. adj.* mild, complaisant.

719. **raconteur** *n.*—an interesting storyteller.

720. **radical** *n., adj.* (*n.* radicalism)—one who favors drastic or revolutionary social, political or other changes; basic. *Syn. adj.* sweeping extreme, immoderate. *Ant. adj.* moderate, temperate, reactionary, conservative.

721. **rambunctious** *adj.*—unruly and noisy. *Syn. adj.* boisterous, uproarious. *Ant. adj.* tranquil, orderly.

722. **ramification** *n.* (*v.* ramify)—a branch of a larger entity. *Syn. n.* subdivision, offshoot.

723. **rampant** *adj.*—unchecked and spreading. *Syn. adj.* unbridled, uncurbed, widespread.

724. **rancid** *adj.*—stale; repulsive in odor due to decay. *Syn. adj.* rank.

725. **rankle** *v.*—to fester or cause increasing mental irritation.

726. **rapport** *n.*—a close, harmonious relationship.

727. **rational** *adj.*—reasonable; sound in judgment. *Syn. adj.* sensible. (**rationale** *n.*—logical explanation or basis.)

728. **raucous** *adj.*—sounding harsh or hoarse.

729. **rebuttal** *n.* (*v.* rebut)—argument or evidence disproving an opponent's point of view, facts, or arguments.

730. **recondite** *adj.*—so profound as to transcend ordinary understanding. *Syn. adj.* abstruse, esoteric, occult. *Ant. adj.* lucid, clear, comprehensible.

731. **redress** *n.*—correction for a wrong inflicted. *Syn. n.* reparation, compensation, indemnity, amends.

732. **regale** *v.*—to entertain or feast lavishly.

733. **regimen** *n.*—a systematic therapy; a course or diet of treatment; an existing system of government. *Syn. n.* regime.

734. **reiterate** *v.* (*n.* reiteration)—to repeat or restate again and again. *Syn. v.* recapitulate, iterate.

735. **remote** *adj.* (*n.* remoteness)—distant in manner, space, time; far away; unlikely. *Syn. adj.* secluded. *Ant. n.* propinquity.

736. **renege** *v.*—to back down on one's word or commitment.

737. **repercussion** *n.*—indirect reaction or echo from an event or action; after-effect. *Syn. n.* reverberation, rebound, recoil.

738. **reprove** *v.* (*n.* reproval)—to express disapproval. *Syn. v.* rebuke,

reproach, chide, censure. *Ant. v.* endorse, sponsor, praise.

739. **resolute** *adj.* (*n.* resolution)—firmly determined. *Ant. adj.* irresolute, wavering, ambivalent.

740. **respite** *n.*—an interval of temporary delay or relief. *Syn. n.* recess, reprieve, postponement, deferment.

741. **restive**—*adj.* restless; impatient; unamenable. *Syn. adj.* untractable, obstinate, balky.

742. **retaliation** *n.* (*v.* retaliate, *adj.* retaliatory)—repayment in kind. *Syn. n.* recrimination (*v.* recriminate), reprisal, requital.

743. **reticent** *adj.* (*n.* reticence)—of silent temperament.

744. **retribution** *n.* (*adj.* retributive, *adj.* retributory)—punishment usually self-inflicted) through repayment; restitution. *Syn. n.* reparation, amends.

745. **retrieve** *v.*—to recover; to regain possession. *Ant. adj.* irretrievable.

746. **revere** *v.* (*adj.* reverential)—to hold in awesome esteem or respect. *Syn. v.* honor, venerate; *n.* reverence.

747. **revive** *v.* (*v.* revivify, *n.* revival)—to restore to life; to renew. *Syn. v.* resuscitate, revitalize; *n.* renascence.

748. **ricochet** *v.*—to rebound one or more times from a flat surface.

749. **rifle** *v.*—to search thoroughly, stripping of everything by plunder. *Syn. v.* ransack, pillage.

750. **rollicking** *adj.* (*v.* rollick)—boisterously high-spirited; carefree; capering; frolicsome. *Syn. n.* lark, romp.

751. **rote** *n.*—mechanical procedure; unthinking repetition.

752. **rue** *v.* (*adj.* rueful)—to regret; to be penitent; to feel or show sorrow over.

753. **ruminate** *v.*—to deliberate. *Syn. v.* contemplate, reflect, meditate.

754. **rummage** *v.*—to search something through actively to the point of upsetting the contents.

755. **rural** *adj.*—relating to the sparsely inhabited countryside and its people. *Syn. adj.* bucolic, rustic, pastoral. *Ant. adj.* metropolitan, urban.

756. **ruse** *n.*—a skillful trick; crafty deception. *Syn. n.* artifice, wile, stratagem.

757. **rusticate** *v.* (*n.* rustication, *adj.* rustic)— to live in the country.

758. **ruthless** *adj.*—merciless; cruel. *Syn. adj.* uncompassionate, unrelenting, ferocious, barbarous. *Ant. adj.* clement, compassionate.

759. **SACROSANCT** *adj.*—inviolable; very sacred.

760. **sally** *v.*—to set out or leap forth with spirit; to rush forward.

761. **salvage** *v.*—to rescue from destruction for further use.

762. **sanctimonious** *adj.* (*n.* sanctimony)—hypocritically pious or virtuous. (Ironical use: unwarranted assumed immunity to being questioned or opposed.)

763. **sanction** *v.*—to give authoritative permission or approval.

764. **sanctity** *n.*—sacredness; godliness.

765. **sang-froid** *n.*—composure under stress or attack. *Syn. n.* equanimity, poise, aplomb.

766. **sanguinary** *adj.*—bloody; gory.

767. **sanguine** *adj.*—cheerfully self-assured; optimistic; hopeful.

768. **sardonic** *adj.*—bitterly mocking; sneering. *Syn. adj.* sarcastic, scornful, cynical, ironic, caustic, derisive.

769. **sartorial** *adj.*—pertaining to tailoring.

770. **satire** *n.* (*n.* satirist, *adj.* satirical)—a literary work in which the writer uses irony or wit to expose or ridicule folly or wickedness.

771. **savoir-faire** *n.*—social tact; sophistication. *Ant. n.* gaucherie, ineptness, boorishness.

772. **savor** *n.* (*adj.* savory)—a particular, distinctive taste or smell (usually pleasant). *Syn. n.* flavor, relish; *adj.* palatable, piquant. *Ant. adj.* insipid, jejune, rancid, fetid.

773. **scintilla** *n.*—a tiny particle. *Syn. n.* speck, mote, iota.

774. **scourge** *n.*—severe affliction, punishment, or torture.

775. **scurrilous** *adj.* (*n.* scurrility, *n.* scurrilousness)—coarsely abusive and insulting. *Syn. adj.* indecent, vituperative.

776. **sectarian** *n.*—a biased adherent to a particular sect or system of beliefs; narrowly limited in scope or interest. *Syn. adj.* partisan, narrow-minded, parochial. *Ant. adj.* liberal.

777. **sedate** *adj.*—sober in behavior. *Syn. adj.* composed, poised, grave, staid, stern, demure, reserved.

778. **sedentary** *adj.*—given to much sitting or to a vocation requiring sitting exclusively. *Ant. adj.* migratory, peregrinating.

779. **semantics** *n.*—the study of historic or other changes in word meanings.

780. **semblance** *n.*—outward superficial appearance. *Syn. n.* surface, mien, air, show, exterior; *adj.* specious.

781. **shibboleth** *n.*—a party slogan or catch phrase.

782. **shriek** *v.*—to cry out in a grating voice. *Syn. v.* screech, shrill, scream. *Ant. v.* mutter, murmur, whisper.

783. **simper** *v.*—to smile affectedly or self-consciously. *Syn. v.* smirk.

784. **simulate** *v.* (*adj.* simulative)— to pretend; to imitate affectedly. *Syn. v.* dissimulate, counterfeit, sham.

785. **simultaneous** *adj.*—occurring at the same time. *Syn. adj.* synchronous, coexistent, coeval.

786. **sinecure** *n.*—a position involving little or no work.

787. **sinuous** *adj.*—curving and winding; indirect. *Syn. adj.* serpentine, roundabout.

788. **skeptic** *n.* (*adj.* skeptical, *n.* skepticism)—one who is inclined to

doubt or question; one critical and incredulous in attitude. *Ant. adj.* credulous.

789. **skulduggery** *n.* —a craftily dishonorable action; trickery. *Syn. n.* craftiness, deception.

790. **skulk** *v.* —to move about stealthily: to lie concealed in waiting. *Syn. v.* slink.

791. **sleazy** *adj.* —of cheap, thin texture. *Syn.* shoddy, flimsy.

792. **smug** *adj.* (*n.* smugness)—displaying self-satisfaction or assumed superior ability. *Syn. adj.* complacent, self-righteous, jaunty, cocky.

793. **sophistry** *n.* (*n.* sophist)—clever but insincere and fallacious argument used to impress or confuse; intellectual trickery. *Syn. n.* quibbling.

794. **soporific** *adj.* —inducing sleep. *Syn. adj.* sedative (*n.* sedation), drowsy.

795. **sovereign** *n.*, *adj.* (*n.* sovereignty)—monarch; self-governing; possessing supreme and unquestioned authority.

796. **spry** *adj.* (*n.* spryness)—nimble; energetic; brisk.

797. **squalid** *adj.* (*n.* squalor)—filthy and neglected; morally unclean. *Syn. adj.* wretched, sordid, foul, ignoble, degrading. *Ant. adj.* splendid, magnificent.

798. **stagnant** *adj.* (*n.* stagnancy)—lacking normal activity; foul because of extended inactivity.

799. **stark** *adj.* (*n.* starkness)—sheer; utter; harsh; severe; bare; unadorned. *Syn. adj.* barren, dreary, desolate, arrant (downright). *Ant. adj.* embellished, extreme.

800. **status** *n.* —condition of affairs; rank; estimable social position.

801. **stereotype** *n.*, *adj.* —the arch pattern from which copies are made; a duplicate or facsimile; lacking in originality. *Syn. adj.* hackneyed, banal, unoriginal. *Ant. n.* archetype, prototype (an original mold), matrix.

802. **stigmatize** *v.* (*n.* stigma)—to mark as disgraceful or dishonorable; to brand.

803. **stodgy** *adj.* (*n.* stodginess)—dull; unimaginative; boring; consciously formal.

804. **stolid** *adj.* (*n.* stolidity)—impassive; not easily excitable. *Syn. adj.* phlegmatic, languid. *Ant. adj.* irascible.

805. **stratum** *n.* (*pl.* **strata**)—a social level; a layer of material. (**stratify** *v.* —to set into different levels of status or privilege.)

806. **stricture** *n.* —an adverse remark, comment, or criticism.

807. **strident** *adj.* (*n.* stridency)—having a grating, harsh sound. *Syn. adj.* creaking. *Ant. adj.* dulcet, mellifluous.

808. **stringent** *adj.* (*n.* stringency)—severely exacting; strict. *Syn. adj.* inflexible, rigid, drastic, compelling, urgent. *Ant. adj.* lenient, lax, permissive, liberal, mild.

809. **stultify** *v.* —to render foolish or absurd.

810. **suave** *adj.* (*n.* suavity)—polished; sophisticated. *Syn. adj.* urbane,

smooth, gracious, worldly. *Ant. adj.* crude, rustic, naive, ingenuous.

811. **subjugate** *v.* (*n.* subjugation)—to conquer; to bring under domination. *Syn. v.* subdue, enslave, vanquish.

812. **subversive** *adj.* (*v.* subvert; *n.* subversion)—undermining or overturning (an existing government).

813. **sultry** *adj.*—uncomfortably hot and moist. *Syn. adj.* humid, sweltering.

814. **sumptuous** *adj.*—luxurious; lavishly expensive.

815. **supersede** *v.*—to replace (someone) in authority or position. *Syn. v.* supplant, displace, succeed.

816. **surcease** *v.*—to stop; to cease from an activity. *Syn. v.* desist; *n.* cessation.

817. **surfeit** (*n., v.*)—excess; to fill to excess; to satisfy beyond ordinary need. *Syn. n.* disgust (due to excess), superfluity; *v.* satiate, saturate, sate (*n.* satiety), imbue, cloy, glut. *Ant. n.* moderation, abstemiousness, temperance; *v.* deplete.

818. **surmise** *v.*—to guess; to conjecture. *Syn. v.* suppose, speculate.

819. **surveillance** *n.* (*n.* surveillant)—close watch kept over a person or place, especially under suspicion. *Syn. n.* reconnaissance, espionage, vigilance, supervision.

820. **swarm** *v.*—to congregate in large numbers. *Syn. v.* overrun, thrive, teem, abound, throng.

821. **swarthy** *adj.*—dark-complexioned. *Syn.* dusky.

822. **syndrome** *n.*—collective traits making up a social condition or disease.

823. **synthesis** *n.* (*v.* synthesize)—combination into one unit of component elements. *Syn. n.* consolidation, fusion, pattern. *Ant. n.* analysis, dissection.

824. **TACIT** *adj.*—not expressed but understood or implied; silent. *Syn. adj.* inferred, implicit.

825. **taciturn** *adj.* (*n.* taciturnity)—customarily silent or uncommunicative. *Syn. adj.* reticent, noncommittal, reserved.

826. **tangible** *adj.*—capable of being touched or felt; discernible; substantial. *Syn. adj.* palpable, corporeal, real, concrete, appreciable. *Ant. adj.* visionary, imaginary, imperceptible.

827. **tantalize** *v.*—to excite one's expectations by teasing or holding out of reach the desired objective.

828. **tantamount** *adj.*—equivalent to in effect or significance.

829. **tantrum** *n.*—a burst of ill temper or violent rage.

830. **taunt** *v.*—to reproach by mockery or ridicule. *Syn. v.* twit, jeer, deride, scoff.

831. **tedious** *adj.* (*n.* tedium)—boring; tiresome; monotonous. *Syn. adj.* wearisome.

832. **teetotaler** *n.*—one who abstains from alcoholic beverages.

833. **temerity** *n.*—reckless scorn of danger. *Syn. n.* foolhardiness, rashness, audacity, effrontery. *Ant. adj.* circumspect,

wary, timorous (*n.* timidity).

834. **temporal** *adj.* —worldly; short-lived. *Syn. adj.* secular, transitory, ephemeral. *Ant. adj.* spiritual.

835. **temporize** *v.* (*n.* temporization)—to delay in order to gain time until a favorable advantage arises; to yield to circumstances or conciliate for the sake of convenience or expediency. *Syn. v.* compromise, be expedient.

836. **tenacity** *n.* (*adj.* tenacious)—stubborn persistency. *Syn. n.* perseverance, pertinacity, steadfastness, doggedness; *adj.* retentive (as of memory).

837. **tenebrous** *adj.* —dark; gloomy; dusky.

838. **tenet** *n.* —a principle, opinion, or doctrine. *Syn. n.* dogma, creed.

839. **tentative** *adj.* —provisional; in the nature of an experiment or trial. *Syn. adj.* hesitant, indecisive.

840. **tenure** *n.* —a term during which something is held.

841. **tepid** *adj.* —lukewarm.

842. **termagant** *n.* —a quarreling, nagging woman. *Syn. n.* scold, shrew, virago.

843. **tether** *v.* —to fasten by a rope or chain in order to restrict movement. *Syn. v.* constrain, constrict.

844. **theocracy** *n.* (*adj.* theocratic)—government by religious leaders.

845. **theology** *n.* (*adj.* theological, *n.* theologian)—a study of religion, God, and religious truths; a system of religious ideas or opinions.

846. **theorize** *v.* (*adj.* theoretical)—to speculate; to formulate a theory.

847. **therapeutic** *adj.* (*n.* therapy)—pertaining to treatment or healing of disease. *Syn. adj.* curative.

848. **thesis** *n.* —a proposition submitted for debate or analysis.

849. **thwart** *v.* —to prevent an action; to prevent an accomplishment. *Syn. v.* balk, frustrate, foil, hinder.

850. **tidy** *adj.* (*n.* tidiness)—neat; orderly. *Syn. adj.* trim, spruce, dapper, considerable (as a *tidy* amount) *Ant. adj.* slovenly, sloppy, disorderly, unkempt.

851. **tinge** *n.*, *v.* —a faint color. *Syn. n.* hue, tint.

852. **tirade** *n.* —a long, vehement, abusive speech or denunciation. *Syn. n.* harangue.

853. **titular** *adj.* —in title or name only. *Syn. adj.* nominal.

854. **torpid** *adj.* (*n.* torpor)—sluggish. *Syn. adj.* listless, lethargic, apathetic. *Ant. adj.* concerned, brisk, energetic.

855. **totalitarian** *adj.* (*n.* totalitarianism)—characteristic of a government which is highly centralized, and which outlaws dissent and controls the major activities in society. *Syn. adj.* authoritarian.

856. **toxic** *adj.* (*n.* toxicity)—poisonous.

857. **traduce** *v.* —to speak maliciously. *Syn. v.* asperse, defame, malign, slander, vilify. *Ant. v.* laud, eulogize.

858. **tranquil** *adj.* (*n.* tranquillity, *v.* tranquilize)—peaceful; calm. *Syn.*

adj. unruffled, placid, halcyon, serene. *Ant. adj.* turbulent, chaotic, tumultuous, riotous.

859. **transcend** *v.* (*adj.* transcendent)—to proceed beyond; to rise above in excellence. *Syn. v.* surpass, exceed, outdo.

860. **transgress** *v.* (*n.* transgressor, *n.* transgression)—to sin; to violate a law; to pass beyond established limits. *Syn. v.* trespass, infringe.

861. **transient** *adj.*—having a short existence or stay. *Syn. adj.* fleeting, momentary, temporary, transitory (short-lived).

862. **transition** *n.* (*adj.* transitional)—passage from one state or position to another.

863. **transparent** *adj.* (*n.* transparency)—(a) admitting passage of light; (b) easily or obviously comprehended, detected, or rendered clear; obvious. *Syn. adj.* (a) translucent, sheer, luminous; (b) lucid, enlightened, intelligible. *Ant. adj.* opaque.

864. **trauma** *n.* (*adj.* traumatic *v.* traumatize)—an enduring mental effect from a previous shocking experience.

865. **travail** *n.*—tremendous, painful, mental or physical agony or toil.

866. **tremulous** *adj.* (*n.* tremor)—trembling; vibrating. *Syn. adj.* quivering, timorous, quavering, oscillating.

867. **trenchant** *adj.*—incisive or cogent in language. *Syn. adj.* caustic, sharp, cutting, clear-cut, forceful. *Ant. adj.* turgid, temperate.

868. **trepidation** *n.*—agitation stemming from fear; quivering alarm. *Syn. n.* perturbation.

869. **trivia** *n., pl.*—an assortment of inconsequential odds and ends; trivialities.

870. **truculent** *adj.* (*n.* truculence) (a) *adj.* savage; brutal. (b) *adj.* inclined to fight. *Syn.* (a) *adj.* scathing, vitriolic; (b) *adj.* pugnacious, bellicose. *Ant. adj.* pacific, pacifist, amicable, conciliatory.

871. **turbid** *adj.* (*n.* turbidity)—muddy; unclear. *Ant. adj.* limpid, transparent.

872. **turbulent** *adj.* (*n.* turbulence)—very agitated or upset. *Syn. adj.* tumultuous, chaotic; *n.* commotion.

873. **turpitude** *n.*—depraved or base conduct; loose, unconformist morals.

874. **tycoon** *n.*—a wealthy, influential industrialist.

875. **typhoon** *n.*—a violent tropical hurricane.

876. **UGLY** *adj.*—displeasing to look at; base; morally objectionable. *Syn. adj.* unsightly, repulsive, uncomely, homely, reprehensible, monstrous.

877. **ukase** *n.*—an arbitrary official proclamation. *Syn. n.* edict, fiat.

878. **ulterior** *adj.*—going beyond the explicit intention or statement.

879. **umbrage** *n.*—hurt pride; resentment. *Syn. n.* pique, inward irritation, offense.

880. **uncanny** *adj.*—mysteriously wonderful or skilled. *Syn. adj.* preternatural, weird.

881. **unconscionable** *adj.*—unscrupulous; immoderately unreasonable; unmoved by conscience. *Syn. adj.* outrageous.

882. **uncouth** *adj.*—crude; boorish. *Syn. adj.* awkward, unrefined. *Ant. adj.* couth, sophisticated; *n.* savoir-faire.

883. **unctuous** *adj.* (*n.* unction)—extravagantly suave, smooth, or pious.

884. **undue** *adj.* (*adv.* unduly)—unsuitably excessive. *Ant. adj.* due (warranted, fitting).

885. **unfathomable** *adj.*—incomprehensible; beyond effective scrutiny. *Syn. adj.* inscrutable. *Ant. adj.* fathomable.

886. **ungainly** *adj.* (*n.* ungainliness)—clumsy, tactless. *Syn. adj.* gauche, awkward.

887. **unison** *n.*—harmony; agreement. *Syn. n.* accord, concordance. *Ant. n.* discord.

888. **unrestrained** *adj.*—uncurbed. *Syn. adj.* unbridled, unchecked, wanton.

889. **unsociable** *adj.*—disinclined to sociability. *Syn. adj.* uncongenial, reserved, reclusive. *Ant. adj.* gregarious, companionable.

890. **unspeakable** *adj.*—highly or inexpressibly objectionable. *Syn. adj.* unutterable.

891. **untenable** *adj.*—incapable of being defended. *Syn. adj.* irrefutable, indefensible. *Ant. adj.* tenable.

892. **unwary** *adj.*—incautious. *Syn. adj.* indiscreet, rash. *Ant. adj.* circumspect.

893. **unwieldy** *adj.*—too bulky to manipulate or manage easily.

894. **unwitting** *adj.*—unintentional; unaware. *Syn. adj.* heedless, inadvertent.

895. **upbraid** *v.*—to censure; to rebuke severely. *Syn. v.* castigate, reprove.

896. **upheaval** *n.*—a violent overturn; a major disruption.

897. **urban** *adj.*—pertaining to one, or a group of, joined metropolitan areas.

898. **urbane** *adj.* (*n.* urbanity)—polished in manners and grace. *Syn. adj.* suave, cosmopolitan, affable.

899. **usurp** *v.* (*n.* usurper, *n.* usurpation)—to seize or appropriate without legal authority. *Syn. v.* sequester; *n.* aggression, expropriation.

900. **usury** *n.* (*adj.* usurious)—excessive interest exacted on a loan.

901. **utopian** *adj.* (*n.* utopia)—involving visionary concepts of an unattainable perfection.

902. **VAGARY** *n.*—an extravagant or odd notion; a flight of fancy. *Syn. n.* caprice, quirk, whim.

903. **vagrant** *n.* (*n.* vagrancy)—a tramp; a wanderer having neither a permanent domicile nor a livelihood. *Syn. n.* rover, vagabond, itinerant.

904. **valedictory** *adj.* (*n.* valedictorian)—in the nature of bidding farewell.

905. **valid** *adj.* (*n.* validity)—sound; reasonable; logical. (**validate** *v.*—to confirm an authorized sanction; to render valid.)

906. **vanguard** *n.*—forefront, as in a political movement or intellectual activity. *Syn. n.* avant-garde.

907. **vantage** *n.*—a point or position giving one superiority or advantage or a wider view or outlook.

908. **vaunt** *v.* (*adj.* vaunted)—to talk boastfully; to display proudly. *Syn. v.* brag; *adj.* vainglorious; *n.* bravado, braggadocio.

909. **vehement** *adj.* (*n.* vehemence)—forceful; furious; raging; extraordinarily fervent.

910. **venal** *adj.* (*n.* venality)—corrupt; accessible to bribery; mercenary.

911. **veneer** *n.*—surface polish or appearance; a superficially good appearance.

912. **venerable** *adj.* (*v.* venerate)—meriting deep respect (usually because of age or achievement). *Syn. adj.* reverential, deferential.

913. **venial** *adj.*—pardonable, the offense being regarded as minor. *Syn. adj.* excusable. *Ant. adj.* mortal.

914. **verbiage** *n.*—excessive use of words. *Syn. n.* wordiness, verbosity.

915. **verdant** *adj.*—green (usually with vegetation). *Syn. n.* verdure.

916. **verisimilitude** *n.*—likelihood; the quality of being true.

917. **veritable** *adj.*—true; actual; genuine.

918. **vernacular** *n., adj.*—the standard unliterary language used by natives in a particular place; the language peculiar to a special group; common parlance.

919. **versatile** *adj.* (*n.* versatility)—apt in a variety of ways; multi-talented.

920. **vertigo** *n.* (*adj.* vertiginous)—dizziness.

921. **verve** *n.*—liveliness of spirit or imagination.

922. **vestige** *n.* (*adj.* vestigial)—a visible trace of a lost thing; remains of a degenerating object.

923. **vex** *v.* (*n.* vexation, vexatious)—to irritate; to provoke; to agitate.

924. **viable** *adj.* (*n.* viability)—capable of being put into practice or action, or of living or developing. *Syn. adj.* practicable, feasible.

925. **vicarious** *adj.*—imaginatively or actually participating sympathetically in another's experience.

926. **vicissitudes** *n.*—the ups and downs in changes of fortune.

927. **vie** *v.* (*pres. part.* **vying**)—to compete for superiority. *Syn. v.* rival.

928. **vile** *adj.* (*n.* vileness)—disgusting; decidedly unpleasant; base. *Syn. adj.* depraved, ignoble, loathsome, abominable.

929. **vindictive** *adj.* (*n.* vindictiveness)—maliciously revengeful;

bitterly retaliatory. *Syn. adj.* vengeful, retributive. *Ant. adj.* forgiving, relenting, extenuating, condoning.

930. **violate** *v.* (*n.* violation)—to break (a law); to desecrate. *Syn. v.* transgress, profane.

931. **virile** *adj.* (*n.* virility)—manly. *Syn. adj.* vigorous.

932. **virtuoso** *n.* (*n.* virtuosity)—a skillful or accomplished artist; expertly skilled. *Syn. n.* connoisseur. *Ant. n.* neophyte, tyro, beginner, novice.

933. **virulent** *adj.* (*n.* virulence)—bitterly antagonistic; hateful; caustic. *Syn. adj.* venomous, vicious, acrimonious.

934. **vitiate** *v.*—to render useless or invalid; to corrupt morally; to spoil. *Syn. v.* impair, pervert, debase.

935. **vitriolic** *adj.*—excessively caustic or biting. *Syn. adj.* scathing, virulent.

936. **vituperation** *n.* (*v.* vituperate, *adj.* vituperative)—verbal abuse or harshness. *Syn. v.* berate, censure, vilify.

937. **vivacious** *adj.* (*n.* vivaciousness, *n.* vivacity)—lively in speech, manner, or action. *Syn. adj.* animated, sprightly.

938. **vociferous** *adj.* (*v.* vociferate, *n.* vociferation)—crying out noisily or vehemently; clamorous. *Syn adj.* blatant, uproarious, boisterous.

939. **volatile** *adj.* (*n.* volatility)—unstable; changing erratically. *Syn. adj.* fickle, inconstant, explosive.

940. **voluble** *adj.* (*n.* volubility)—readily talkative. *Syn. adj.* loquacious, glib, fluent.

941. **vulgar** *adj.* (*n.* vulgarity, *n.* vulgarian)—lacking in refinement or good taste in speech, dress, manners. *Syn. adj.* boorish, crude, indelicate, garish. (**vulgarism** *n.*—a colloquial, coarse expression.)

942. **vulnerable** *adj.* (*n.* vulnerability)—defenseless; conquerable. *Ant. adj.* impregnable, invincible.

943. **WAN** *adj.*—sickly pale from an emotional distress or after an illness. *Syn. adj.* pallid, ashen. *Ant. adj.* ruddy, rubicund.

944. **wanton** *adj.* (*n.* wantonness)—(a) sexually unrestrained. (b) done without justification or provocation. (c) extravagantly luxurious; giving freely. *Syn. adj.* (a) loose, lewd, libidinous, dissolute, lustful; (b) calculated, heedless, malicious; (c) lavish.

945. **wastrel** *n.*—a spendthrift. *Syn. adj.* prodigal, dissolute, idling.

946. **wayward** *adj.*—erratic; unpredictable; capricious, perverse or willfully disobedient. *Syn. adj.* contrary, refractory, intractable. *Ant. adj.* constant, conformist, amenable.

947. **weighty** *adj.*—(a) burdensome; (b) of utmost importance; (c) carrying considerable weight, force, or influence. *Syn. adj.* (a) oppressive, ponderous; (b) significant, momentous; (c) effective.

948. **weird** *adj.* (*n.* weirdness)—strange; unearthly. *Syn. adj.* odd,

eerie, uncanny, fantastic. *Ant. adj.* natural.

949. **wheedle** *v.*—to induce or persuade by flattery, deception, or coaxing. *Syn. v.* cajole, inveigle, beguile.

950. **whim** *n.* (*adj.* whimsical, *n.* whimsy)—a sudden fancy or impulse. *Syn. n.* caprice, quirk, vagary, oddity, humor.

951. **whimper** *v.*—to cry in a whining voice.

952. **wicked** *adj.* (*n.* wickedness)—evil doing or minded (immoral); vicious; pernicious; sinful (unrighteous). *Syn. adj.* heinous, flagitious, depraved, iniquitous (impious).

953. **willful** *adj.* (*n.* willfulness)—disobedient; insistent on imposing one's own will. *Syn. adj.* headstrong, perverse.

954. **wily** *adj.* (*n.* wiliness)—having or using wile or cunning. *Syn. adj.* sly, artful, guileful.

955. **winsome** *adj.* (*n.* winsomeness)—engagingly pleasant.

956. **wistful** *adj.* (*n.* wistfulness)—evincing hope or longing in a melancholy manner. *Syn. adj.* pensive.

957. **witless** *adj.*—stupid; without wit.

958. **wizen** *v.* (*adj.* wizened)—to shrivel. *Syn. v.* wither; *adj.* shrunken.

959. **wrangle** *v.*—to quarrel; to dispute in an unruly way. *Syn. v.* brawl, bicker.

960. **wrath** *n.* (*adj.* wrathful)—rage. *Syn. n.* fury, resentment.

961. **wrest** *v.*—to seize or usurp forcibly; to obtain by twisting violently.

962. **writ** *n.*—a written court order, opinion or summons.

963. **XENOPHOBIA** *n.* (*n.* xenophobe)—a contempt for, or fear and hatred of foreigners.

964. **YOKE** *n.*—(literally) a contrivance joining a pair of draft animals to a plow; (figuratively) any form of servitude. *Syn. n.* bondage, subjugation.

965. **ZANY** *n.*, *adj*—clown, simpleton. *Syn. n.* buffoon.

966. **zeal** *n.* (*adj.* zealous, *n.* zealot)—great fervor or enthusiasm; fanaticism.

967. **zenith** *n.*—the highest point or degree of attainment. *Syn. n.* summit, peak, acme, culmination. *Ant. n.* nadir, abyss.

968. **zephyr** *n.*—a gentle wind.

A Glossary of Vogue Words and Expressions

The following words have had popular currency in newspapers and other mass media as well as in textbooks, novels, and the daily reading students are faced with. Naturally, therefore, they are bound to appear in the vocabulary sections of college entrance and other aptitude examinations.

969. **activist** *n.*—an energetic participant in a cause; an advocate of vigorous action to achieve a social or political aim.

970. **ad infinitum** *adv.* —without a calculable stop; endlessly.
971. **ambience** *n.* —complete surroundings; the spirit or act of an environment; milieu.
972. **amnesty** n.—pardon given officially to an offender against the laws of war.
973. **apartheid** *n.* – racial segregation, especially in South Africa.
974. **aura** *n.* —a distinctive spirit or character emanating from a person or surroundings.
975. **avant-garde** *n.* —a person or group which applies new, original, or experimental artistic or intellectual ideas; the vanguard of any intellectual or artistic movement.
976. **backlash** *n.* —a sudden often explosive reaction to a plan for reform or pacification.
977. **brainwash** *v.* —indoctrinate; to attempt through long indoctrination to induce someone to give up basic political, social, or religious beliefs and attitudes and to accept contrasting ones.
978. **chutzpah** *n.* (Yiddish) – shameless impudence or boldness.

979. **colonialism** *n.* —a policy of maintaining sovereign authority over another people or territory.
980. **condominium** *n.* —individual ownership of an apartment in a building or a complex of buildings.
981. **confrontation** *n.* —a face-to-face meeting of active opponents with a view to defying, exploring, and possibly settling their differences.
982. **credibility gap** *n.* – an inconsistency between a person's stated pledge or statement and the actual truth, often resulting in damage to that person's reputation for truthfulness.
983. **disaffected** *adj.* —alienated; estranged, commonly from traditional standards, ideas, or programs.
984. **embargo** *n.* —a legal or other restriction or prohibition imposed upon commerce.
985. **expose** *n.* —a public disclosure of a secret, discreditable act.
986. **input** *n.* —data put into a computer; a contribution to effectuate a proposed plan or program.
987. **missile** *n.* —a projectile type of war weapon.
988. **monitor** *n.* —a device used to keep close surveillance or check on broadcasts, propaganda, plots, and censorable messages.
989. **nationalization** *n.* —legal or arbitrary expropriation by a government of industries, land, or alien industries and properties within its territory.
990. **negotiation** *n.* (*v.* negotiate, *adj.* negotiable)—a meeting between representatives of contesting parties in an endeavor by discussion and dickering to arrive at a settlement of their differences.
991. **persona non grata** *n.* —an emissary, diplomatic representative, or

any other person who is regarded with disfavor or is unacceptable to the government to which he is accredited.

992. **prima facie** *adj.*—literally, at first sight; based on immediate impression.

993. **profile** *n.* – a vivid biographical sketch of an individual, accentuating personality and character.

994. **recession** *n.*—a temporary reduction in general economic activity, marked by a decline in employment, profits, production, and sales.

995. **scenario** *n.*—a detailed working outline or synopsis of the plot of a dramatic work.

996. **schizophrenia** *n.*—a mental disorder characterized by a split in personality.

997. **summit** *n.*—a meeting between chiefs of state or heads of government of two countries in order to improve relations.

998. **tokenism** *n.* (*n.* token)—the symbolic admittance of a limited number of minority members of society into schools or businesses as in compliance with the civil rights law.

999. **urban renewal** *n.*—rehabilitation of dilapidated city areas.

1000. **value judgment** *n.*—a judgment reflecting one's personal view.

COLLEGE ENTRANCE
SCHOLASTIC APTITUDE TESTS

APTITUDE TEST ONE

PART *A* — SYNONYMS AND ANTONYMS

Time: 30 Minutes

I. *Directions:* In each group below, you will find a capitalized word followed by five words or expressions numbered (1) to (5). Choose the word or expression that is most nearly *similar* in meaning to the capitalized word.

1. FALLIBLE — (1) likely to err (2) unsteady (3) illogical (4) unsuccessful (5) jocose

2. CHIMERICAL—(1) prosaic (2) fantastic (3) scientific (4) melodious (5) facetious

3. MUNDANE — (1) spiritual (2) pecuniary (3) worldly (4) munificent (5) begrudging

4. FECUND — (1) sparse (2) conspiratorial (3) embarrassed (4) unimpressive (5) prolific

5. URBANE — (1) metropolitan (2) polished (3) witty (4) pastoral (5) meek

6. WRANGLE — (1) change (2) brawl (3) vex (4) design (5) mangle

7. ALTRUISTIC — (1) skeptical (2) egotistical (3) unselfish (4) philosophical (5) concerned

8. EXPURGATE — (1) obliterate (2) quell (3) alleviate (4) intercept (5) cleanse

9. DISDAIN — (1) haughtiness (2) prevarication (3) synthesis (4) avowal (5) disavowal

10. IMPECCABLE — (1) aloof (2) culpable (3) sorry (4) blameless (5) fraudulent

11. OPULENT — (1) stealthy (2) furtive (3) wealthy (4) grotesque (5) popular

12. PITHY — (1) pathetic (2) commodious (3) prolix (4) nutritious (5) concise

APTITUDE TEST ONE

13. ZENITH — (1) lowest point in the heavens (2) facsimile (3) heavens (4) epitaph (5) culmination

14. IMPECUNIOUS — (1) indigent (2) unsystematic (3) indigenous (4) peremptory (5) humorless

15. TEMPORIZE — (1) defer (2) prevaricate (3) economize (4) heat (5) anticipate

16. GARISH — (1) adorned (2) awkward (3) noisy (4) showy (5) freakish

17. MOOT — (1) confused (2) debatable (3) legalistic (4) unsymmetrical (5) habitual

18. INVETERATE — (1) novice (2) recalcitrant (3) recumbent (4) confirmed in habit (5) vulgar

19. VORACITY — (1) truth (2) lack of moderation (3) cupidity (4) vengeance (5) temerity

20. RETALIATION — (1) retribution (2) summary (3) dictum (4) exposition (5) incursion

21. NEBULOUS — (1) heavenly (2) contradictory (3) shiny (4) hazy (5) lucid

22. PECCADILLO — (1) blame (2) onus (3) foible (4) criticism (5) pettiness

23. LANGUID — (1) sleazy (2) sophisticated (3) oily (4) leathery (5) lacking in spirit

24. AMBIGUOUS — (1) deceptive (2) vague (3) hypocritical (4) false (5) incorrect

25. EXPUNGE — (1) ruin (2) quash (3) ostracize (4) delete (5) impose upon

26. CHICANERY – (1) intoxication (2) daring (3) duplicity (4) extravagance (5) urbanity

27. PROPITIOUS — (1) favorable (2) remote (3) near (4) flattering (5) thoughtful

28. GREGARIOUS — (1) perfunctory (2) sociable (3) abbreviated (4) prohibited (5) curt

29. MEANDERING — (1) walking (2) running (3) skipping (4) uncertain (5) winding and turning

30 QUACK — (1) alarm (2) mountebank (3) harsh tone (4) connoisseur (5) dilettante

II. *Directions:* In each group below, you will find five words numbered (1) to (5). Choose two words in each group that are most nearly *similar or opposite* to each other in meaning.

1. (1) clement (2) mendacious (3) mendicant (4) inexorable (5) unwieldy

2. (1) longevity (2) taciturnity (3) transitoriness (4) transmutation (5) curtailment

3. (1) cantankerous (2) complaisant (3) recondite (4) complacent (5) complimentary

4. (1) intrepid (2) pusillanimous (3) candid (4) cogent (5) expeditious

5. (1) urbane (2) pastoral (3) boorish (4) animalistic (5) fertile

6. (1) obese (2) vaunted (3) gossamery (4) gaunt (5) obtrusive

7. (1) dispassionate (2) illustrious (3) impecunious (4) affluent (5) hypercritical

8. (1) efface (2) censure (3) oscillate (4) rescind (5) expunge

9. (1) vapid (2) spurious (3) piquant (4) ostentatious (5) equivocal

10. (1) heterodox (2) paradox (3) cynicism (4) skepticism (5) traditional

11. (1) indolent (2) innuendo (3) condolence (4) dolorous (5) slothful

12. (1) incredulous (2) atheistic (3) esoteric (4) epicurean (5) gullible

13. (1) maladroit (2) queer (3) fervent (4) gauche (5) sinister

14. (1) augment (2) prognosticate (3) evade (4) amplify (5) segregate

15. (1) bigoted (2) enigmatic (3) bucolic (4) pellucid (5) stoical

16. (1) avid (2) exotic (3) bizarre (4) expatriated (5) erring

17. (1) characterization (2) climax (3) epithet (4) pulchritude (5) castigation

18. (1) dubious (2) vociferous (3) flamboyant (4) raucous (5) tepid

19. (1) eminent (2) impending (3) erudite (4) infallible (5) learned

20. (1) censurable (2) inadvertent (3) unknown (4) productive (5) thoughtless

APTITUDE TEST ONE

21. (1) sovereign (2) congenial (3) incompatible (4) indomitable (5) hospitable

22. (1) irascible (2) serene (3) heretical (4) verbose (5) opinionated

23. (1) increment (2) trivia (3) erratum (4) stipend (5) compensation

24. (1) perverse (2) tractable (3) adverse (4) averse (5) dogmatic

25. (1) antipathy (2) versatility (3) derivative (4) precursor (5) harbinger

26. (1) inquiring (2) querulous (3) questionable (4) petulant (5) trivial

27. (1) authoritative (2) docile (3) refractory (4) radical (5) progressive

28. (1) peremptory (2) perfunctory (3) meticulous (4) rhythmic (5) alliterative

29. (1) banal (2) destructive (3) excluded (4) trite (5) piebald

30. (1) wandering (2) nefarious (3) dull (4) putrid (5) iniquitous

PART *B* — COMPREHENSION

Time: 30 Minutes

Directions: In each selection below, you will find one or more blanks indicating the omission of a word, or a phrase, or a pair of words or phrases which will make the sense complete. Following the selection are five choices numbered (1) to (5). Choose the item that you think will best complete the meaning of the selection.

1. The pleasure of imparting opinions in print is by no means confined to ...., to people who are assumed to know something about a subject because they have been more or less occupied with it for years.

    (1) amateurs (2) heretics (3) dilettantes (4) connoisseurs (5) mystics

2. .... is .... abuse in words.

    (1) eulogy — vituperative (2) criticism — impartial (3) vituperation — strong (4) allusion — impartial (5) criticism — vituperative

3. The fox is a very wild and suspicious creature, but . . . ., when it is held by a trap, or driven by the hound, its expression is not that of fear, but of shame and guilt. It seems to diminish in size and to be overwhelmed with humiliation.

(1) naturally   (2) curiously enough   (3) to be sure   (4) innocently enough   (5) true to its nature

4. A person who is free from . . . . is said to be . . . .

(1) calumny — innocent   (2)   matrimony — domesticated   (3) bias — arbitrary   (4) bigotry — opinionated   (5) bias — equitable

5. From the days of the earliest explorers, the Missouri has been known as a wild river – ungovernable, unpredictable, almost unnavigable. Yet. . . . . people have never ceased to set their craft upon its . . . . waters.

(1) docile — tranquil   (2) obdurate – turbulent   (3) pertinacious — elusive   (4) adventurous — calm   (5) stubborn — unfathomable

6. One wonders why so many critics have spent countless years trying to decipher the works of writers who lived long before the birth of Christ which on the very face betray evidence of being frauds. Giving these works meticulous examination has seldom led to creditable conclusions about either the character of the authors or the times in which they lived. One should like to remind these critics that a(n) . . . . piece of literature is one that is not . . . .

(1) spurious — unauthentic   (2) genuine — authentic   (3) apocryphal — authentic   (4) creditable — unauthentic   (5) autobiographical — biased

7. Red squirrels are as . . . . as chipmunks. They lay up stores . . . ., by fits and starts; they never have enough put up to carry them over the winter; hence they are more or less active all the season.

(1) improvident — regularly   (2) impudent — irregularly   (3) unostentatious — systematically   (4) improvident — irregularly   (5) calculating — punctilious

8. Every fourth autumn the United States policy in foreign affairs becomes the subject of vigorous . . . . fervor. The public halls resound with the dire warnings or the fulsome praise mouthed by speakers who twist logic to suit their purpose and who use reasoning that is obviously . . . .

(1) partisan — sound   (2) non-partisan — plausible   (3) forensic — specious   (4) specious — hysterical   (5) preposterous — callous

9. Matters which are too profound for popular understanding may be termed ....

> (1) abstruse   (2) pellucid   (3) flagitious   (4) obtuse   (5) perspicuous

10. The atmosphere of this historical volume is so convincing; the penetration into the mysteries and only half-tamed terrors of the primitive mind so accurate; the understanding of Gaul, Rome, Syria, and other ancient lands so complete; and the .... of all the many-sided people who parade through this book so excellent that it should .... every lover of imaginative exploration into the past except those who merely want to be entertained.

> (1) analysis — alienate   (2) diffusiveness — attract   (3) paradox — displease   (4) characterization — please   (5) portraiture — ostracize

11. Where Thackeray is ...., Dickens is idealistic; where the former dissects the foibles and the duplicity of society, the latter weeps for the .... of the lower classes. The one is sorry for the human race; the other asks the reader to extend a helping hand to the improvident, the oppressed, and the derelict.

> (1) emotional—eccentricities   (2) cynical—frailties   (3) romantic — triumphs   (4)   skeptical — virtues   (5)   banal — commonplaces

12. Nelly Bly did splendid work in uncovering the desperate conditions that faced the one-third of a nation of her time. On the Pittsburgh paper where she got her start she wrote .... articles that attacked the complacency which she found in the industrial age that surrounded her. The smug rulers of the industrial world were in their heyday when Nelly lived. With a missionary zeal she .... their selfishness, their limitless opulence, their apathy to the sufferings of the underprivileged classes.

> (1) fiery — eulogized   (2) insipid — magnified   (3) soporific — castigated   (4) esoteric — deprecated   (5) fiery — castigated

13. A large part of our current slang is propagated by the newspapers, and much of it is .... by newspaper writers. One need but turn to the slang of baseball to find numerous examples. Such phrases as *to clout the sphere. the initial sack, to slam the pill*, and the *dexter meadow* are .... not of bleachers' manufacture. There is not enough imagination in that depressing army to devise such things; more often than not, there is not even enough intelligence to comprehend them. The true place of their origin is the perch of the newspaper reporters, whose competence and compensation is largely estimated, at least on papers of wide circulation, by their capacity for inventing novelties.

(1) eschewed — definitely   (2)   vitiated — unquestionably   (3) invented — obviously   (4) decried — obviously   (5) perverted — obviously

14. Though fond of many acquaintances, I desire an intimacy only with a few. The man in black whom I have often mentioned is one whose friendship I could wish to acquire, because he possesses my esteem. His manners, it is true, are tinctured with some strange inconsistencies; and he may be justly termed a humorist in a nation of humorists. Though he is generous even to profusion, he affects to be thought a prodigy of . . . . and prudence; though his conversation be replete with the most sordid and selfish maxims, his heart is dilated with the most unbounded love. I have known him profess himself a man-hater, while his cheek was glowing with . . . . ; and while his looks were softened with pity, I have heard him use the language of the most unbounded ill-nature.

(1)   munificence — revulsion   (2)   parsimony — animosity   (3) garrulity — compassion   (4) parsimony — compassion   (5) condolence — niggardliness

15. No sensible person will lightly counter an opinion firmly held by a great body of his countrymen. He will take for granted, that for any opinion which has struck deep root among a people so powerful, so successful, and so well worthy of respect as the people of this country, there certainly either are, or have been, good and sound reasons. He will venture to . . . . such an opinion with real hesitation, and only when it appears that the reasons which once supported it exist no longer, or at any rate seem about to disappear very soon.

(1) impugn   (2)   trust   (3)   confirm   (4)   criticize   (5)   place credence in

16. This is a book for the years. For one thing, it is a distinguished job of writing, made so by Paula Keene's skill as a narrator, her powers as a penetrative analyst and her ingrained habit of viewing . . . . any idea so long popular that it is accepted as truth. The . . . . of soldiers and the platitudes of politicians do not awe her. What tradition seems to confirm she accepts provided it meets the test of logic. This persistent, often eloquent attack on slogans and on half-truth should delight all students of military affairs.

(1)   credulously — maxims   (2)   fearfully — truths   (3)   incredulously — paradoxes   (4) skeptically — shibboleths   (5) curiously — challenges

APTITUDE TEST ONE

17. A(n) .... is a(n) ....
situation.

    (1) paradox — weird   (2) crisis — unfathomable   (3) analogy —
reasonable   (4) anomaly — irregular   (5) heterodox—untenable.

18. To .... is to evade the truth by ....

    (1) circumvent — insinuating   (2) quibble — procrastinating   (3)
temporize — circumspection   (4) prevaricate — quibbling   (5)
equivocate — temporizing

19. Short poems that are very popular and so are frequently mentioned
become hackneyed; and then we are in danger of thinking them ....
.... But if a poem is very popular because it is very
good, its becoming hackneyed for us is entirely our affair. It remains what
it was, but we through our weakness cannot get at it. I have met people
who .... as hackneyed *Break, break, break,* and
Crossing the Bar; and doubtless, if they cannot read these poems freshly,
they do well not to read them at all. But for the poems themselves, I think
they are as sure of immortality as anything in the language.

    (1) insipid — eulogized   (2) commonplace — decried   (3) notori-
ous — reproached   (4) racy — construed   (5) exceptional — dep-
recated

20. A person who is affectedly .... may be
said to be ....

    (1) conceited — demure   (2) frivolous — garish   (3) taciturn —
garrulous   (4) reticent — bumptious   (5) modest — demure

PART *C*

Time: 30 Minutes

I. Analogies

> *Directions:* In each group below, you will find two capitalized words
> which bear a certain logical relationship to each other. These are
> followed by five pairs of words numbered (1) to (5). Choose the
> pair of words which have the same relationship to each other as do
> the capitalized words.

1. HIDE : SHOE : :   (1) fur : animal   (2) sand : cement   (3) pulp :
volume   (4) cloth : coat   (5) wool : sheep

2. CANDIDATE : ELECTION : :   (1) statesman : peace   (2) pilot :
skill   (3) refugee : asylum   (4) plotter : stratagem   (5) sprinter
: **gun**

3. ZEPHYR : CYCLONE : : (1) breeze : hurricane   (2) rage : ire
(3) typhoon : storm   (4) impulse : outburst   (5) tantrum : rage

4. MIND : VACILLATION : :   (1) body : quiver   (2) wind : rustle
(3) vagrant : fancy   (4) mood : caprice   (5) boat : adrift

5. ASSUME : KNOW : :   (1) hypothesize : assume   (2) theorize :
calculate   (3) conjecture : surmise   (4) suppose : think   (5) hypothesis : knowledge

6. CLIMAX : DRAMA : :   (1) denouement : novel   (2) crisis : disease   (3) corner : road   (4) terminal : crossways   (5) plot :
mystery

7. CHAOS : ANARCHY : :   (1) laxity : terror   (2) tyranny : disorder
(3) order : control   (4) force : violence   (5) pandemonium : ruth-
lessness

8. DEVIOUS : FORTHRIGHT : :   (1) surreptitious : accurate   (2)
secretive : aboveboard   (3) circumvent : forestall   (4) indirect :
circuitous   (5) detour : meander

9. INSINUATE : CHARGE : :   (1) inform : suggest   (2) intimate :
innuendo   (3) imply : infer   (4) hint : allege   (5) divulge : disclose

10. MARE : STALLION : : (1) heifer : cow   (2) colt : filly   (3) buck:
deer   (4) cow : bull   (5) lamb : sheep

11. EULOGY : CREDITABLE : :   (1) consecration : idealistic   (2)
opprobrium : egregious   (3) approbation : nefarious   (4) glorification : deed   (5) castigation : ignominious

12. TROWEL : MASON : :   (1) cue : billiards   (2) awl : plumber
(3) quill : priest   (4) tool : craftsman   (5) adz : carpenter

13. MUNIFICENT : GENEROUS : :   (1) patron : benefactor   (2)
lavish : liberal   (3) opulent : philanthropic   (4) unsparing : parsimonious   (5) free : uninhibited

14. CRYPTIC : ENIGMATIC : :   (1) acrostic : obtuse   (2) recondite :
connoisseur   (3) funereal : mysterious   (4) verbose : prolix   (5)
terse : trite

15. AFFECTATION : SIMPLICITY : :   (1) dowager : matron   (2)
ostentation : artlessness   (3) elegant : refined   (4) artful : artless
(5) love : humility

16. OBSESSION : INTEREST : :   (1) fascination : influence   (2) infatuation : love   (3) prepossession : engagement   (4) animation :
callousness   (5) thrill : perturbation

17. ZENITH : CAREER : : (1) nadir : pinnacle (2) struggle : culmination (3) crest : wave (4) altitude : mountain (5) epitome : beauty

18. ORANGE : WHEEL : : (1) fruit : wagon (2) sphere : circle (3) cylinder : circle (4) plane : sphere (5) ellipsis : round

19. KNOWLEDGE : ERUDITE : : (1) proficiency : esoteric (2) scholarship : learned (3) industry : indolent (4) profundity : lucid (5) dexterity : manual

20. TRAITOR : OSTRACISM : : (1) infidel : skepticism (2) sluggard : emulation (3) villain : approbation (4) turncoat : remorse (5) renegade : banishment

21. DERELICT : OBLIGATION : : (1) punctilious : schedule (2) appointment : prompt (3) cursory : perusal (4) thorough : dilatoriness (5) remiss : duty

22. SOLILOQUY : CONVERSATION : : (1) discourse : chat (2) confession : sermon (3) dialogue : duet (4) duet : solo (5) monologue : colloquy

23. EXTIRPATE : ENGENDER : : (1) incarcerate : emancipate (2) curb : encourage (3) prohibit : inhibit (4) quell : quash (5) mother : child

24. PRESUMPTION : MODESTY : : (1) modesty : pride (2) haughtiness : meticulousness (3) laconic : diffidence (4) aggressiveness : prudery (5) arrogance : reserve

25. COSMOPOLITAN : PAROCHIAL : : (1) boorish : crude (2) abstemious : gluttonous (3) sophisticated : enlightened (4) urbane : boorish (5) equitable : dogmatic

II. Antonyms

Directions: In each group below, you will find a capitalized word followed by five words or expressions numbered (1) to (5). Choose the word or expression that is most nearly *opposite* in meaning to the capitalized word.

1. CRAVEN — (1) valiant (2) animated (3) pusillanimous (4) desirous (5) abstemious

2. MOLLIFY — (1) surreptitious (2) aggravate (3) allay (4) weaken (5) disqualify

3. OBLIVIOUS — (1) aware (2) hidden (3) unmindful (4) grotesque (5) perfervid

4. DELETERIOUS — (1) apparent (2) calm (3) salutary (4) unavoidable (5) muddy

5. INTRACTABLE — (1) accountable (2) baneful (3) incompatible (4) docile (5) truculent

6. HYPERBOLE — (1) square (2) elliptical (3) exaggeration (4) exoticism (5) verisimilitude

7. IMPERVIOUS — (1) blocked (2) permeable (3) transitional (4) meek (5) envious

8. MENDICANT — (1) truthful (2) irreparable (3) procrastinating (4) philanthropic (5) parsimonious

9. REPRISAL — (1) retaliation (2) acquiescence (3) lachrymose (4) lack of expectation (5) eulogy

10. SAGACITY — (1) mildness (2) sapience (3) obtuseness (4) futility (5) cynicism

11. EFFETE — (1) ineffective (2) dismal (3) remote (4) prolific (5) imagistic

12. EQUIVOCAL — (1) disparaging (2) unbiased (3) answerable (4) evasive (5) straightforward

13. FRUSTRATE — (1) discomfit (2) renege (3) construct (4) abet (5) baffle

14. INERT — (1) dynamic (2) oppressive (3) nerveless (4) resistant (5) crotchety

15. PEREMPTORY — (1) active (2) incontrovertible (3) inclusive (4) indecisive (5) apparent

16. VIRULENT — (1) benign (2) unmanly (3) free from disease (4) feminine (5) disparaging

17. EXONERATE — (1) acquit (2) revenge (3) include (4) convict (5) infect

18. DEMURE — (1) decisive (2) emancipated (3) mural (4) diffident (5) immodest

19. TACITURN — (1) miserly (2) verbose (3) fallible (4) humorless (5) expressive

20. INORDINATE —(1) scant (2) moderate (3) numerous (4) immeasurable (5) orderly

APTITUDE TEST TWO

PART *A* — SYNONYMS AND ANTONYMS

Time: 30 Minutes

I. *Directions:* In each group below, you will find words numbered (1) to (5). Select the two words in the group that are most nearly *similar or opposite* to each other in meaning.

1. (1) plausible (2) vindictive (3) discreditable (4) reasonable (5) extrinsic

2. (1) sully (2) petrify (3) sally (4) defile (5) hibernate

3. (1) pacified (2) recoiled (3) rapacious (4) predatory (5) anachronistic

4. (1) ominous (2) redolent (3) auspicious (4) unsuspecting (5) revolting

5. (1) extenuated (2) extinct (3) extent (4) extroverted (5) extant

6. (1) manly (2) virulent (3) noxious (4) pervasive (5) clean

7. (1) raw (2) precocious (3) obsolete (4) retarded (5) chastened

8. (1) curtailed (2) sinuous (3) evil (4) protracted (5) irrevocable

9. (1) jaunty (2) mellifluous (3) sardonic (4) impaled (5) cacophonous

10. (1) inference (2) reduction (3) deduction (4) allegation (5) extemporization

11. (1) fugitive (2) religious (3) parsimonious (4) corrupt (5) magnanimous

12. (1) inane (2) dictatorial (3) harmonious (4) didactic (5) fatuous

13. (1) disparity (2) equanimity (3) arbitrariness (4) equality (5) querulousness

14. (1) feasible (2) fickle (3) indecisive (4) lugubrious (5) capricious

15. (1) depreciate (2) implore (3) apprehend (4) deprecate (5) deplore

16. (1) transient   (2) inveterate   (3) corporeal   (4) indistinguishable
(5) impasse

17. (1) understatement   (2) hyperbole   (3) devilish   (4) elliptical   (5)
insinuation

18. (1) mangled   (2) maudlin   (3) prolix   (4) reserved   (5) antipathetic

19. (1) incumbent   (2) recumbent   (3) cumbrous   (4) gossamer   (5)
moot

20. (1) conduit   (2) derelict   (3) vagary   (4) idiosyncrasy   (5) motley

21. (1) licentious   (2) dull   (3) unrestrained   (4) illegal   (5) rote

22. (1) elfin   (2) devoted   (3) impious   (4) imperfect   (5) devout

23. (1) arterial   (2) venal   (3) altruistic   (4) craven   (5) grotesque

24. (1) palliate   (2) heinous   (3) hackneyed   (4) deceive   (5) hoodwink

25. (1) unprejudiced   (2) equivocal   (3) frank   (4) caustic   (5) hostile

26. (1) functional   (2) perfunctory   (3) cursory   (4) curt   (5) fatuous

27. (1) similar   (2) plagiaristic   (3) literal   (4) lateral   (5) metaphorical

28. (1) futile   (2) effective   (3) effete   (4) protuberant   (5) stimulating

29. (1) propulsion   (2) partiality   (3) effusion   (4) promontory   (5)
precipice

30. (1) meritorious   (2) meretricious   (3) specious   (4) duality   (5)
insignificant

II. *Directions:* In each group below, you will find a capitalized word
followed by five words numbered (1) to (5). Choose the word or
expression that is most nearly *opposite* in meaning to the capitalized
word.

1. BELLICOSE — (1) unfavorable   (2) peaceful   (3) unintelligible
(4) ugly   (5) ungainly

2. HETERODOX — (1) skeptical   (2) ominous   (3) traditional   (4)
platitudinous   (5) serene

3. IMMUTABLE — (1) changeable   (2) constant   (3) quixotic   (4)
invariable   (5) nebulous

4. BUMPTIOUS — (1) contumelious   (2) irritable   (3) devious   (4)
retiring   (5) sparing

APTITUDE TEST TWO

5. FIASCO — (1) success   (2) eulogy   (3) lowest point   (4) impassivity   (5) steadiness

6. MURKY — (1) tenebrous   (2) clear   (3) sultry   (4) fulgent   (5) inexplicable

7. SATIATED — (1) universal   (2) unsatisfactory   (3) famished   (4) glutted   (5) horizontal

8. MITIGATE — (1) dispatch   (2) intensify   (3) release   (4) accept   (5) deny

9. TIMOROUS — (1) rash   (2) valiant   (3) untimely   (4) traditional   (5) wretched

10. EFFUSIVE — (1) gushing   (2) laconic   (3) mild   (4) fulsome   (5) predictable

11. GREGARIOUS — (1) unsociable   (2) scanty   (3) chanting rhythmically   (4) flagrant   (5) flocking together

12. OSTENSIBLE — (1) passable   (2) frivolous   (3) divisible   (4) actual   (5) visual

13. MARITAL — (1) warlike   (2) peaceful   (3) celibate   (4) nautical   (5) wedded

14. DEVIATE — (1) demur   (2) conform   (3) stray   (4) plot   (5) careen

15. OBDURATE — (1) stubborn   (2) defiant   (3) disdainful   (4) yielding   (5) contemptible

16. CRYPTIC — (1) disinterred   (2) concise   (3) evasive   (4) inept   (5) enigmatic

17. ADULATION — (1) senescence   (2) approbation   (3) contempt   (4) embolism   (5) virtue

18. VACILLATION — (1) constancy   (2) appeasement   (3) vigor   (4) stiffen   (5) autocracy

19. OBSEQUIOUS — (1) ingratiating   (2) neglectful   (3) transparent   (4) disdainful   (5) courageous

20. GUILELESS — (1) arty   (2) artful   (3) artless   (4) articulate   (5) not gullible

21. SORDID — (1) dolorous   (2) vile   (3) pleasant   (4) gruesome   (5) impenitent

22. RESILIENT — (1) recriminatory   (2) refractory   (3) flexible   (4) compliant   (5) inelastic

23. DISPASSIONATE — (1) emotional (2) oblivious (3) passive (4) condoned (5) reputable

24. AFFECTED — (1) flippant (2) sincere (3) arrogant (4) despicable (5) villainous

25. DOWDY — (1) tidy (2) slatternly (3) mighty (4) vulnerable (5) discreditable

26. UNWARY — (1) deceitful (2) circumvented (3) precluded (4) circumspect (5) incurable

27. SOVEREIGN—(1) resigned (2) contingent (3) penniless (4) obstinate (5) dependent

28. PENCHANT — (1) prone (2) disinclination (3) supine (4) adverse (5) suspension

29. INERT — (1) willing (2) dynamic (3) phlegmatic (4) abated (5) heedless

30. NOVICE — (1) amateur (2) antiquarian (3) shibboleth (4) commoner (5) virtuoso

PART *B* — SYNONYMS

Time: 30 Minutes

I. *Directions:* In each group below, you will find a capitalized word followed by five words or expressions numbered (1) to (5). Choose the word or expression that is most nearly *similar* in meaning to the capitalized word.

1. ABERRANT — (1) affirmative (2) precocious (3) abnormal (4) punitive (5) correct

2. ESCHEW — (1) catch cold (2) delete (3) avoid (4) disinherit (5) masticate

3. INNOCUOUS — (1) innocent (2) harmless (3) helpless (4) noisome (5) objectionable

4. ENNUI — (1) annoyance (2) excitement (3) destruction (4) boredom (5) depletion

5. ANATHEMA — (1) malediction (2) sedative (3) framework (4) lineage (5) benediction

6. TALISMAN — (1) juror (2) amulet (3) charlatan (4) aborigine (5) informer

7. FLACCID — (1) horizontal (2) flaky (3) lute-like (4) limp (5) scourged

8. INDUBITABLE — (1) without doubt (2) able to be coupled (3) impious (4) distrustful (5) skeptical

9. SYCOPHANT — (1) pleasure-seeker (2) hypochondriac (3) toady (4) autocrat (5) emperor

10. CABAL — (1) strong wire (2) find fault (3) cavalier (4) coterie (5) clamor

11. SEDULOUS — (1) seductive (2) diligent (3) gloomy (4) reserved (5) insidious

12. PLAUSIBLE — (1) appealing (2) irrational (3) reasonable (4) entertaining (5) ridiculous

13. CONTINGENT—(1) fortuitous (2) distorted (3) incessant (4) (4) dependent (5) capable of containing

14. TANTAMOUNT — (1) one behind the other (2) sweepstakes (3) wild-cat (4) equivalent (5) excessive

15. ROCOCO — (1) fool (2) game (3) monkey (4) parrot (5) excessively ornamental

16. QUIXOTIC — (1) generous (2) questionable (3) impracticable (4) dangerous (5) dashing

17. PSEUDONYM — (1) alien (2) assumed name (3) nickname (4) signature (5) slogan

18. FRACAS — (1) accident (2) mistake (3) owl (4) brawl (5) stew

19. SYMPTOMATIC — (1) indicative (2) ill (3) fatal (4) devious (5) scientific

20. RELINQUISH — (1) accede (2) abandon (3) deplete (4) forget (5) reminisce

21. PLETHORA — (1) apoplexy (2) sine curve (3) panic (4) epidemic (5) abundance

22. SURCEASE — (1) extra crop (2) remainder (3) transfer (4) treachery (5) respite

23. LOQUACIOUS — (1) taciturn (2) talkative (3) terse (4) laughable (5) contradictory

24. FLAMBOYANT — (1) cheerful (2) inflamed (3) ornate (4) periodic (5) carefree

25. BAYOU — (1) marshy inlet   (2) scream   (3) window frame   (4) infant   (5) emissary

26. DURESS — (1) hard material   (2) compulsion   (3) eternal   (4) duration   (5) hardiness

27. MUNDANE — (1) munificent   (2) pertaining to the mouth   (3) spiritual   (4) worldly   (5) financial

28. SPLENETIC — (1) gorgeous   (2) laxative   (3) of the kidneys   (4) peevish   (5) unaccented

29. LUGUBRIOUS — (1) burdensome   (2) sad   (3) stout   (4) emaciated   (5) spirited

30. INSIPID — (1) tasteless   (2) succulent   (3) dripping   (4) vacillating   (5) inactive

II. *Directions:* In each group below, you will find two capitalized words which bear a certain logical relationship to each other. These are followed by five pairs of words numbered (1) to (5). Choose the pair of words which have the same relationship to each other as do the capitalized words.

1. PERSONALITY : TRAITS : : (1) aspect : question   (2) character : ideals   (3) disposition : attitudes   (4) criticism : discussion   (5) outlook : point of view

2. SHOE : SPIKE : : (1) head : bullet   (2) sled : runner   (3) handle : fork   (4) prong : fork   (5) pin : head

3. EARTH : SUN : : (1) satellite : planet   (2) follower : leader   (3) spoke : wheel   (4) hand : dial   (5) electron : atom

4. LADDER : RUNG : : (1) incident : plot   (2) climax : episode   (3) stairway : step   (4) mountain : peak   (5) reputation : fame

5. VAULT : COMBINATION : : (1) plot : climax   (2) knowledge : book   (3) knot : string   (4) house : doorbell   (5) lock : key

6. COPPER : MALLEABLE : : (1) resilient : rubber   (2) iron : solid   (3) cork : lightness   (4) wood : transparent   (5) rubber : elastic

7. MISANTHROPE : MANKIND : : (1) philanthropist : charity   (2) celibate : marriage   (3) hydrophobia : dogs   (4) misogynist : woman   (5) pyromaniac : fire

APTITUDE TEST TWO

8. RAZE : RAISE : : (1) synonym : homonym   (2) hail : hale   (3) efface : mar   (4) expunge : delete   (5) extirpate : construct

9. RADICAL : LIBERAL : : (1) zealot : fanatic   (2) insurgent : rebel   (3) conservative : reactionary   (4) reactionary : conservative   (5) progressive : liberal

10. EMULATE : EXEMPLARY : : (1) feign : deceptive   (2) eschew : delectable :   (3)   collude : fraudulent   (4)   scorn : depraved   (5) descry : raucous

11. MOMENTOUS : PALTRY : : (1)   prodigious : insignificant   (2) presently : trifling   (3) time : extent   (4) prodigal : lavish   (5) contemporary : posterior

12. AUTHENTIC : SPURIOUS : : (1) apocryphal : genuine   (2) genuine : sham   (3) pseudonym : anonymous   (4) mountebank : veritable   (5) hero : imposter

13. CONDOLE : GRIEF : : (1) aggravate : misery   (2) soothe : balm   (3) condone : success   (4) commiserate : adversity   (5) forbear : misfortune

14. ADAMANT : APPEAL : : (1) inexorable : plea   (2) implacable : fault   (3) callous : pleasure   (4) ruthless : arrogance   (5) haughty : meek

15. SELDOM : OFTEN : : (1) infrequent : sometimes   (2)   never : hardly   (3) sporadically : infrequently   (4) rarely : infrequent   (5) uncommonly : repeatedly

16. QUELL : RIOT : : (1) dispel : doubt   (2) quash : insurgency   (3) intensify : holocaust   (4) compound : collusion   (5) connive : fraud

17. PROVERB : PLATITUDE : : (1) paradox : anomaly   (2) maxim : epigram   (3) pithy : banal   (4) insipid : pungent   (5) bromide : epigram

18. FAWNING : CIVIL : : (1) cringing : cowering   (2) flattering : praising   (3) affable : courteous   (4) obsequious : affable   (5) vile : humble

19. CONFORM : TRADITION : : (1) subservient : master   (2) subdue : adversary   (3) observe : ritual   (4) intensify : preparation   (5) obligation : reject

20. REDOUBTABLE : FEAR : : (1) credulous : doubt   (2) irascible : anger   (3) charitable : awe   (4) querulous : response   (5) mendacious : distrust

21. PILFER : FUNDS : : (1) procrastinate : time   (2)   dissipate : energies   (3) abscond : responsibility   (4) plagiarize : ideas   (5) parody : songs

22. RIOT : REBELLION : : (1) quarrel : misunderstanding   (2) discord : panacea   (3) retribution : reprisal   (4) disorder : pandemonium   (5) dissent : chaos

23. RENEGADE : OSTRACIZE : : (1) minority : quell   (2) pariah : emancipate   (3) disfranchise : felon   (4) misdemeanor : chasten   (5) traitor : expatriate

24. GENIALITY : POPULARITY : : (1) intelligence : obtuseness   (2) courage : indecisiveness   (3) moroseness : friendlessness   (4) friendlessness : indifference   (5) joy : exultation

25. CANTANKEROUS : EQUABLE : : (1) crotchety : just   (2) biased : unbiased   (3) petulant : peevish   (4) testy : even-tempered   (5) unequal : equal

PART *C* — COMPREHENSION

Time: 30 Minutes

Directions: In each selection below, you will find one or more blanks indicating the omission of a word, or a phrase, or a pair of words or phrases which will make the sense complete. Following the selection are five choices numbered (1) to (5). Choose the item that you think will best complete the meaning of the selection.

1. Perhaps the best way to describe Addison's peculiar pleasantry is to compare it with the pleasantry of some other great satirists. The three most eminent masters of the art of .... during the eighteenth century, were, we conceive, Addison, Swift, and Voltaire. Which of the three had the greatest power of moving laughter may be questioned. But each of them, within his own domain, was ....
....

(1) acrimony — notorious   (2) banter — ludicrous   (3) raillery — preeminent   (4) notoriety — acrimonious   (5) skepticism — supreme

2. Abstracts, abridgments, and ...., have the same use with burning glasses — to .... diffused rays of wit and learning in authors and make them point with warmth and quickness upon the reader's imagination.

(1) expositions – spread (2) synopses – augment (3) harangues – scatter (4) compendiums – collect (5) anthologies – intensify

APTITUDE TEST TWO

3. The commentators on Homer apologize for the glaring ....
.... which Ulysses relates, by showing that these fabrications
are told to the Phoenecians, a(n) .... people.

(1)   prevarications — credulous   (2)   prevarications — incredible
(3) prognostications —obtuse   (4) truths — veracious   (5) hyper-
boles — cynical

4. Hitler was not the .... but the product of the
anti-democratic .... that swept through Europe
after the First World War.

(1) culmination — holocaust   (2) precursor — holocaust   (3) nadir
— frenzy   (4)   initiator — parsimony   (5)   paragon — histrionics

5. Alexander the Great, reflecting on his friends degenerating into ....
.... and luxury, told them that it was a most slavish
thing to luxuriate, and a most royal thing to ....

(1)   industry — rest   (2)   indolence — equivocate   (3)   sloth —
labor   (4) perseverance — rest   (5) assiduity — idle

6. Goldsmith lived in what was intellectually by far the best society
of the kingdom, in a society in which no talent or accomplishment was
wanting, and in which the art of conversation was cultivated with splendid
success. There probably were never four talkers more admirable in four
different ways than Johnson, Burke, Beauclerc, and Garrick; and Goldsmith was on terms of intimacy with all the four. He aspired to share in
their .... renown; but never was ambition more
unfortunate. It may seem .... that a man who
wrote with so much perspicuity, vivacity, and grace, should have been,
whenever he took a part in conversation, an empty, noisy, blundering
rattle.

(1)   political — abstruse   (2)   conjectural — odd   (3)   dubious —
paradoxical   (4) didactic — natural   (5) colloquial — strange

7. The .... is sure of everything, and the
.... believes nothing.

(1)   skeptic — dogmatist   (2)   dogmatist — skeptic   (3)   pedant
— credulous   (4) dogmatist — opinionated   (5) skeptic — fool

8. Whatever may be the merits of the English in all the other sciences,
declares Goldsmith, they seem particularly excellent in the art of healing.
There is scarcely a disorder incident to humanity against which our
advertising doctors are not possessed with a most infallible ....

(1) anecdote   (2) antidote   (3) sinecure   (4) opprobrium   (5)
odium

9. Objects near our view are apt to be thought greater than those of a larger size that are more ....; and so it is with pleasure and pain; the present is apt to carry it, and those at a distance are apt to be .... to it.

(1) approximate — partial   (2) remote — oblivious   (3) egregious — hostile   (4) oblivious — remote   (5) remote — apprehensive

10. There are two things which ought to teach us to think little of human glory: the very best have had their ...., the very worst their ....

(1) novices — panacea   (2) panegyrists — calumniators   (3) calumniators — panegyrists   (4) epitomes — epithets   (5) apathy — indifference

11. Friendship improves happiness and .... misery by doubling our joy and dividing our grief.

(1) abates   (2) abets   (3) intensifies   (4) augments   (5) amplifies

12. The surest way of governing, both in a private family and in a kingdom, is for a parent and a ruler sometimes to drop their ....
....

(1) indigence   (2) parsimony   (3) affability   (4) prerogative   (5) folly

13. The greatest person is one who chooses right with the most invincible resolution; who resists the sorest temptation from within and without; who bears the heaviest burden cheerfully; who is calmest in storms, and most .... under menaces and challenges.

(1) intrepid   (2) fearful   (3) querulous   (4) acquiescent   (5) dolorous

14. Habit, if wisely and .... formed, becomes truly a second nature, as the common saying is; but unskilfully and .... directed, it will be as it were the ape of nature, which imitates nothing to the life, but only clumsily and awkwardly.

(1) perfunctorily — methodically   (2) methodically — punctiliously   (3) skillfully — desultorily   (4) carefully — prudently   (5) heedlessly — desultorily

15. The rogue was such a master of the art of .... in which he so much excelled, that people were not ashamed to be deceived even a second time by him.

(1) veracity   (2) aptitude   (3) dissimulation   (4) candor   (5) prognostication

APTITUDE TEST TWO

16. .... is public ....

    (1) eulogy — opprobrium (2) obloquy — adulation (3) effrontery — notoriety (4) calumny — hyperbole (5) ignominy — dishonor

17. To .... is to increase a person's ....

    (1) delineate — grandeur (2) exacerbate — bitterness (3) expatiate — stature (4) exonerate — guilt (5) placate — esteem

18. True friends visit us in prosperity only when invited, but in .... they come without invitation.

    (1) adversity (2) vagary (3) vicissitude (4) atavism (5) disparity

19. A person customarily given to .... may be termed ....

    (1) voracity — mendicant (2) veracity — mendacious (3) falsehood — mendacious (4) magnanimity — venal (5) altruism — mercenary

20. An action done in a .... manner is committed ....

    (1) plausible — furtively (2) frustrating — warily (3) expeditious clandestinely (4) furtive — covertly (5) feasible — plausibly

APTITUDE TEST THREE

PART *A* — SYNONYMS AND ANTONYMS

Time: 30 Minutes

I. *Directions:* In each group below, you will find five words numbered (1) to (5). Choose two words in each group that are most nearly *similar or opposite* to each other in meaning.

1. (1) farrago (2) entreaty (3) edict (4) sovereignty (5) decree

2. (1) precarious (2) nefarious (3) vicarious (4) contemptuous (5) contumelious

3. (1) pithy (2) protuberant (3) prolix (4) ephemeral (5) benign

4. (1) indignant (2) indigent (3) indigenous (4) impecunious (5) sparse

5. (1) pungent (2) perfunctory (3) nettled (4) punctilious (5) punctual

6. (1) delinquent (2) metaphorical (3) discerning (4) literal (5) gregarious

7. (1) diverse (2) averse (3) reverse (4) fain (5) adverse

8. (1) hibernal (2) diurnal (3) nocturnal (4) autumnal (5) harmless

9. (1) effectual (2) effervescent (3) barren (4) prolific (5) antagonistic

10. (1) corroborate (2) gainsay (3) repeat (4) capitulate (5) catastrophic

11. (1) quixotic (2) quintessential (3) feasible (4) rabid (5) precipitous

12. (1) tractable (2) inadvertent (3) imperceptible (4) grandiloquent (5) amenable

13. (1) acrid (2) acerb (3) putrid (4) avid (5) meticulous

14. (1) derisive (2) lachrymose (3) risible (4) relaxed (5) razed

15. (1) integrate (2) palliate (3) soften (4) imprecate (5) adumbrate

16. (1) appreciate (2) deprecate (3) supplicate (4) accentuate (5) approve

APTITUDE TEST THREE

17. (1) refractory   (2) compliant   (3) inexhaustible   (4) devoid   (5) reprehensible

18. (1) remit   (2) admit   (3) submit   (4) capitulate   (5) commit

19. (1) saturnine   (2) taciturn   (3) solemn   (4) solitary   (5) solicitous

20. (1) lubricate   (2) vacillate   (3) concede   (4) persevere   (5) consecrate

21. (1) apothecary   (2) ichthyologist   (3) hedonist   (4) aesthete   (5) ascetic

22. (1) cynic   (2) satirist   (3) pontiff   (4) skeptic   (5) altruist

23. (1) uniform   (2) disparate   (3) cogent   (4) distraught   (5) egregious

24. (1) chary   (2) eleemosynary   (3) implacable   (4) delicate   (5) massive

25. (1) mordant   (2) remorseless   (3) impenitent   (4) impious   (5) discursive

26. (1) tautological   (2) chronic   (3) chromatic   (4) sporadic   (5) anachronistic

27. (1) contiguous   (2) approximate   (3) periphrastic   (4) remote   (5) mottled

28. (1) hopeful   (2) sanguinary   (3) sporadic   (4) prolific   (5) occasional

29. (1) delineate   (2) expound   (3) sketch   (4) allude   (5) exude

30. (1) devious   (2) flippant   (3) visible   (4) indirect   (5) tenuous

II. *Directions:* In each group below, you will find a capitalized word followed by five words or expressions numbered (1) to (5). Choose the word or expression that is most nearly *opposite* in meaning to the capitalized word.

1. SURREPTITIOUS — (1) covert   (2) vulnerable   (3) acquiescent   (4) latent   (5) overt

2. PRECARIOUS — (1) invaluable   (2) paltry   (3) worthless   (4) secure   (5) gainful

3. BELLICOSE — (1) thin   (2) putrid   (3) pacific   (4) modest   (5) truculent

4. EFFUSIVE — (1) curt   (2) restricted to one locality   (3) apparent   (4) **parsimonious**   (5) cumulative

5. INHERENT – (1) intrinsic (2) extrinsic (3) loosely held (4) closely held (5) exiled

6. ASTUTE — (1) dishonorable (2) courageous (3) obtuse (4) wary (5) incredulous

7. PRIMORDIAL – (1) bland (2) biting (3) modern (4) archaic (5) chaotic

8. LAX — (1) assiduous (2) profuse (3) lawful (4) willing (5) apathetic

9. PRECIPITATE – (1) temerarious (2) valiant (3)cautious (4) insolent (5) postdated

10. PROPITIOUS — (1) shallow (2) low (3) penurious (4) inauspicious (5) mitigating

11. SPURIOUS — (1) open-minded (2) clandestine (3) inadvertent (4) indolent (5) authentic

12. CALUMNY — (1) praise (2) unbleached (3) refutation (4) contradiction (5) criticism

13. SOPHISTICATED — (1) iniquitous (2) glamorous (3) naive (4) demented (5) cosmopolitan

14. FLIPPANT — (1) devious (2) flagrant (3) earnest (4) honest (5) mocking

15. GAINSAY — (1) confirm (2) defend (3) alter (4) speak in monotone (5) avoid

16, EQUIVOCAL — (1) unequal (2) implicit (3) unambiguous (4) unbiased (5) biased

17. INCORPOREAL — (1) solitary (2) substantial (3) immaterial (4) dependent (5) disorganized

18. JEJUNE — (1) senescent (2) young (3) aged (4) insipid (5) satisfying

19. PERFIDIOUS — (1) steadfast (2) imperfect (3) connubial (4) lack of fealty (5) ugly

20. VERACITY — (1) lack of color (2) dissimulation (3) emulation (4) lack of appetite (5) starving

21. WRANGLING — (1) concord (2) lavish giving (3) whispering (4) raucousness (5) rancor

22. LUMINOUS — (1) stark (2) murky (3) wan (4) lurid (5) unsensational

APTITUDE TEST THREE

23. MALEVOLENCE — (1) happiness   (2) disdain   (3) benevolence   (4) peace   (5) lack of understanding

24. FICKLE — (1) unassuming   (2) not feasible   (3) constant   (4) mercurial   (5) saturnine

25. TREPIDATION — (1) pusillanimity   (2) confidence   (3) crassness   (4) palpitation   (5) integrity

26. CONTINGENT — (1) independent   (2) unrelated by blood   (3) irritable   (4) uncontained   (5) unrestrained

27. SALUBRIOUS — (1) not salty   (2) salutatory   (3) rough   (4) noxious   (5) innocuous

28. PHLEGMATIC — (1) disinterested   (2) cursory   (3) healthy   (4) perfervid   (5) certain

29. AVARICE — (1) courage   (2) insipidity   (3) cupidity   (4) lack of greed   (5) solidity

30. SURFEIT — (1) abstinence   (2) satiety   (3) underestimate   (4) capitulate   (5) initiate

PART *B* — COMPREHENSION

Directions: In each selection below, you will find one or more blanks indicating the omission of a word, or a phrase, or a pair of words or phrases which will make the sense complete. Following the selection are five choices numbered (1) to (5). Choose the item that you think will best complete the meaning of the selection.

1. A thing that is free from .... is ....

(1) bias — incontrovertible   (2) credence — creditable   (3) error — impeccable   (4) fault — fallible   (5) error — errant

2. Mr. Churchill, few would ...., stands among the world's great figures. The qualities of such great people most frequently include wide-ranging interests and abilities, and high productivity. In this framework Mr. Churchill's life works are not unusual in scope and quantity. He has simply worked away with the .... and effectiveness of those of his caliber. A random look through the pages of history at some of these individuals whom we consider giants will document the point.

(1) interpolate – procrastination   (2) avouch – indolence   (3) asseverate – irascibility   (4) deny – diligence   (5) gainsay – dilatoriness

3. But at its best, the intellectual's concern for coherence, logic and consistency performs an indispensable and long-range service. For it encourages him to cut beneath the surface and to put his finger on potential trouble. He is the diagnostician of the .... disorders of a society. And this is why he is not likely to have anything to say in an election year which will make either party very happy.

(1) universal (2) manifest (3) latent (4) overt (5) conspicuous

4. Thomas Jefferson — a(n) .... man who seemed to be actively interested in everything — turned his hand, and turned it well, at being a parliamentarian, diplomat, city planner, monetary systematizer, vicarious explorer, philosopher, scientist, scholar, architect, agronomist, and, along with Voltaire, one of the most .... correspondents. Fifty-odd volumes of his writings are being edited at Princeton University under the supervision of Julian P. Boyd.

(1) provincial — reticent (2) reserved — discursive (3) versatile — prolific (4) inscrutable — diligent (5) vociferous — avid

5. Mr. Compton tells, and tells well, the story of how, with his .... encouragement, the brilliant team under the late Enrico Fermi brought about the first nuclear chain reaction. He recalls the .... of top-level advisers in Washington when he reported his decision to carry out this hazardous experiment in the midst of populous Chicago.

(1) unwavering — jubilation (2) erratic — encouragement (3) occasional — horror (4) unflagging — consternation (5) incongruous — vacillation

6. Chesterton loved to write with tongue in cheek. He took a rogue's delight in making the absurd sound ....

(1) irrational (2) abstruse (3) jocund (4) nebulous (5) plausible

7. A question that is subject to .... may be said to be ....

(1) dispute — impromptu (2) equivocation — moot (3) controversy — moot (4) debate — irrefutable (5) hysteria — equivocal

8. In all true tragedy there is an element of the unresolved and the unexplained. Oedipus and Hamlet are tragic figures because we are never certain whether they are victims of Fate and the Gods or victims of themselves. And in the case of O'Neill's best plays there is always a similar .... In some of the earlier, like *The Hairy Ape* and *All God's Chillun Got Wings*, one possible interpretation is sociological and economic. In *Strange Interlude* and *Mourning Becomes Electra*, it is Freudian. But in no case is this interpretation the only possible one.

(1) platitude (2) certitude (3) prerogative (4) ambiguity **(5)** authenticity

9. To .... is to indicate a(n) .... course.

(1) prevaricate — dubious (2) prognosticate — questionable **(3)** circumvent — indirect (4) frustrate — alternate (5) prognosticate — future

10. The two most precious things on this side of the grave are our reputation and our life. But it is to be .... that the most contemptible whisper may deprive us of the one, and the weakest weapon of the other. The wise, therefore, will be more anxious to deserve a fair name than to possess it, and this will teach them so to live as not to be .... to die.

(1) lamented — fain (2) noteworthy — glad (3) diverting — afraid (4) deplored — afraid (5) regretted — unafraid

11. We talk of human life as a .... ; but how variously is that journey performed! There are those who come forth girt, and shod, and mantled, to walk on velvet lawns and smooth terraces, where every gale is arrested and every beam tempered. There are others who walk on the Alpine paths of life, against driving misery, and through stormy sorrows, over sharp .... ; walk with bare feet and naked breast, jaded, mangled, and chilled.

(1) performance — auspices (2) paragon — successes (3) vicissitude — precipices (4) peregrination — respites (5) peregrination — tribulations

12. Philosophers say that human beings constitute a ...., or little world, resembling in miniature every part of the great; and the body natural may be compared to the body politic.

(1) macrocosm (2) paroxysm (3) prelude (4) microcosm **(5)** fiasco

13. All the poets are indebted more or less to those who have gone before them; even Homer's originality has been questioned, and Virgil owes almost as much to Theocritus in his *Pastorals*, as to Homer in his *Heroics;* and if our own countryman, Milton, has soared above both Homer and Virgil, it is because he has .... some feathers from their wings. But Shakespeare stands alone. His want of ....

was almost happy and productive ignorance; it forced him back upon his own resources, which were exhaustless.

(1) purloined — erudition   (2) contributed — scholarship   (3) borrowed — magnanimity   (4) augmented — originality   (5) detected — duplication.

14. A great estate is a great disadvantage to those who do not know how to use it, for nothing is more common than to see wealthy persons live scandalously and miserably. . . . . does not serve them as a means of obtaining virtue and happiness. Therefore it is precept and principle, not an estate, that makes a person good for something.

(1) opulence   (2) affectation   (3) impecuniosity   (4) parsimony   (5) indigence

15. A person of few words can never be accused of being . . . ., nor can the person of many be stigmatized as . . . .

(1) reticent — saturnine   (2) acrimonious — garrulous   (3) pithy — terse   (4) loquacious — laconic   (5) platitudinous — paradoxical

16. In our time, the audience of a member of Parliament is the nation. The three or four hundred persons who may be present while a speech is delivered may be pleased or disgusted by the voice and action of the orator; but, in the reports which are read the next day by hundreds of thousands, the difference between the noblest and the meanest figure, between the richest and the most . . . . tones, between the most graceful and the most . . . . gesture, altogether vanishes. A hundred years ago, scarcely any report of what passed within the walls of the House of Commons was suffered to get abroad.

(1) orotund — fatuous   (2) grandiloquent — raucous   (3) ephemeral — shrill   (4) raucous — uncouth   (5) plebeian — dexterous

17. He is a swarthy man of fifty; well-made and good-looking; with crisp dark hair, bright eyes, and a broad chest. His sinewy and powerful hands, as sunburnt as his face, have evidently been used to a pretty rough life. What is curious about him is that he sits forward in his chair as if he were, from long habit, allowing space for some dress or accoutrements that he has altogether laid aside. His step too is measured and . . . ., and would go well with a weighty clash and jingle of spurs. He is close-shaved now, but his mouth is set as if his upper lip had been for years familiar with a great mustache; and his manner of occasionally laying the open palm of his brown hand upon it, is to the same effect. Altogether one might . . . . Mr. George to have been a trooper once upon a time.

(1) lugubrious — conclude   (2) light — conjecture   (3) weighty — doubt   (4) ponderous — surmise   (5) unsubstantial — resolve

18. Not a breath of air stirred over the free and open prairie: the clouds were like light piles of cotton; and where the blue sky was visible, it wore a hazy and .... aspect. The sun beat down upon us with a ...., penetrating heat almost insupportable, and as our party crept slowly along over the interminable level, the horses hung their heads as they waded fetlock deep through the mud, and the men slouched into the easiest position in the saddle.

(1) luminous — murky   (2) translucent — sultry   (3) nebulous — swarming —   (4) languid — luminous   (5) languid — sultry

19. The effect of historical reading is ...., in many respects, to that produced by foreign travel. Readers, like tourists, are transported into a new state of society. They see novel fashions. They hear new modes of laws, or morals, and of manners. But people may travel far, and return with minds contracted as if they never stirred from their own market-town. In the same manner, we may know the dates of many battles, and the .... of many royal houses and yet be no wiser.

(1) anomalous — pleasures   (2) contrary — vicissitudes   (3) analogous—genealogies   (4) identical—sovereignty   (5) diverting—misfortunes

20. The perfect historian is one in whose work the character and spirit of an age is exhibited in miniature. He relates no fact, he attributes no expression to his characters, which is not.................... by sufficient testimony.

(1) authenticated   (2) perverted   (3) refuted   (4) gainsaid   (5) rendered spurious

PART *C*

Time: 30 Minutes

I. Analogies

Directions: Supply the fourth term of the analogy in each of the following groups. Be sure that the term you select from the five choices given below bears the same logical relationship to its partner as does the other pair of words in the completed analogy in capital letters.

1. PROLOGUE : PLAY : : .... : CONSTITUTION

(1) amendment   (2) preamble   (3) epilogue   (4) soliloquy   (5) monologue

2. VINDICATION : INNOCENT : : .... : CUL-
PABLE
(1) allegation   (2) extenuation   (3) condoning   (4) exculpation
(5) conviction

3. LETHARGIC : SLOW : : ENERGETIC : ....
(1) cursory   (2) current   (3) expeditious   (4) dilatory   (5) expedient

4. FRAUGHT : .... : : TEEMING : DEPLETED
(1) prolific   (2) swarming   (3) fecund   (4) eke   (5) devoid

5. ETIQUETTE : DECORUM : : AMENITIES : ....
(1) propriety   (2) enmity   (3) testiness   (4) indecorum   (5) impropriety

6. PRONE : PROCLIVITY : : .... :   REPUG-
NANCE
(1) adverse   (2) supine   (3) averse   (4) apt   (5) partial

7. PLEBISCITE : DEMOCRACY : : WEALTH : ....
**(1) demagoguery   (2) aristocracy   (3) plutocracy   (4) monar-
chy   (5) fascism**

8. GOURMAND : SURFEIT : : .... : SELF-
DENIAL
(1) ascetic   (2) epicurean   (3) stoic   (4) cynic   (5) idealist

9. ABJURE : OATH : : .... : PRINCIPLE
(1) abscond   (2) reaffirm   (3) conform   (4) renounce   (5) avouch

10. AFFECT : FEIGN : : PRESUMPTION : ....
(1) arrogance   (2) apathy   (3) emulation   (4) aggression   (5)
simulation

11. WIT : .... : : JESTER : BUFFOONERY
(1) banter   (2) sarcasm   (3) cynic   (4) folly   (5) ridicule

12. RAM : .... : : DRAKE : DUCK
(1) boar   (2) stallion   (3) ewe   (4) gelding   (5) cockerel

13. .... PRIMEVAL : : MASTODON : DINOSAUR
(1) mammoth   (2) aboriginal   (3) coeval   (4) contemporary   (5)
meridian

14. ADAGIO : ALLEGRO : : .... : MERCURIAL
(1) tempo   (2) cadence   (3) expeditious   (4) saturnine   (5)
velocity

15. COLOSSUS : MANNEQUIN : : .... : EMACIATED
(1) corpulent   (2) microcosmic   (3) pallid   (4) wan   (5) attenu-
ated

16. . . . . : ASSAIL : : IMPREGNABLE : ATTACK
    (1) jeopardy (2) invulnerable (3) ballast (4) controversial
    (5) indefatigable

17. PIRACY : PLAGIARISM : : PILFERAGE : . . . .
    (1) kleptomania (2) megalomania (3) pyromania (4) histri-
    onics (5) larceny

18. HOVEL : . . . . : : PALACE : MAGNIFICENCE
    (1) squalor (2) rococo (3) vulgarity (4) garnished (5) coziness

19. DISINGENUOUS : . . . . : : CANDID : RESPECT
    (1) sycophancy (2) approbation (3) acclamation (4) adulation
    (5) scorn

20. CRUMPLE : FOLD : : SPILL : . . . .
    (1) furrow (2) cut (3) erase (4) pour (5) quell

21. HEREAFTER : THEREAFTER : : . . . . : ENSUE
    (1) eternity (2) follow (3) recede (4) consequently (5) super-
    sede

22. DISAGREEMENT : . . . . : : COMPATIBILITY : CON-
    CORD
    (1) concurrence (2) belligerency (3) accord (4) pandemonium
    (5) felicity

23. REITERATE : RECAPITULATE : : . . . . : RESOUND
    (1) retrench (2) retaliate (3) reverberate (4) revoke (5)
    retrieve

24. PROVINCIAL : RURAL : : METROPOLITAN : . . . .
    (1) urbane (2) bucolic (3) suave (4) sophisticated (5) urban

25. . . . . : EPHEMERAL : : SPIRITUAL : ETERNAL
    (1) diurnal (2) mundane (3) sectarian (4) fleeting (5) celestial

II. Synonyms

Direction: In each group below, you will find a capitalized word fol-
    lowed by five words or expressions numbered (1) to (5). Choose
    the word or expression that is most nearly *similar* in meaning to the
    capitalized word.

1. MEANDERING — (1) muttering (2) aimless wandering (3) pe-
    rusing (4) ejaculating (5) insinuation

2. WARY — (1) slim (2) fearful (3) circumspect (4) bargaining
    (5) peddling

3. PEDANTRY — (1) scholarly achievement   (2) stupidity   (3) undue display of learning   (4) skill in walking   (5) ostentation

4. EDIFY — (1) instruct   (2) horrify   (3) bewilder   (4) prevaricate   (5) construct

5. AMELIORATE — (1) aggravate   (2) amend   (3) belittle   (4) eke   (5) improve

6. INARTICULATE — (1) polylingual   (2) mispronounced   (3) ambiguous   (4) imbue   (5) unable to express oneself

7. EXACERBATE — (1) exaggerate   (2) embitter   (3) tease   (4) wheedle   (5) soften

8. RICOCHET — (1) weave   (2) spray   (3) rebound   (4) wander aimlessly   (5) perambulate

9. GARISH — (1) intensive   (2) gaudy   (3) illiterate   (4) exotic   (5) alien

10. ENTREATY — (1) conference   (2) dialogue   (3) plea   (4) abrogation   (5) understanding

11. PRECURSOR — (1) sovereign   (2) forerunner   (3) posterity   (4) violator   (5) one who curses

12. ACCOLADE — (1) sign of esteem or respect   (2) strong drink   (3) potion   (4) brief speech   (5) harangue

13. GAUCHE — (1) right-handed   (2) ambidextrous   (3) unlucky   (4) gaudy   (5) awkward

14. INNUENDO — (1) insinuation   (2) deference   (3) footnote   (4) procrastination   (5) direct reference

15. NOSTALGIA — (1) panacea   (2) homesickness   (3) bitterness   (4) revulsion   (5) entanglement

16. STEREOTYPED — (1) original   (2) bizarre   (3) hackneyed   (4) depraved   (5) indomitable

17. FORBEARING — (1) prolific   (2) laconic   (3) unrestrained   (4) torpid   (5) restrained

18. CELIBATE — (1) roisterer   (2) drunkard   (3) celebrity   (4) bachelor   (5) clergyman

19. CONFLAGRATION — (1) stealth   (2) hyperbole   (3) fire   (4) conspiracy   (5) inflation

20. INEPT — (1) unskillful   (2) dextrous   (3) heedless   (4) dull   (5) inattentive

APTITUDE TEST THREE

21. DISMAY — (1) rescind   (2) dispel   (3) disfigure   (4) disparage   (5) disconcert

22. GIBE — (1) jeer   (2) compare   (3) imprison   (4) talk loosely   (5) whisper

23. AWRY — (1) mocking   (2) amiss   (3) symmetrical   (4) unauthorized   (5) berserk

24. MORASS — (1) sparseness   (2) swamp   (3) meadow   (4) fog   (5) estuary

25. FETISH — (1) whim   (2) odd remark   (3) objective   (4) object of unreasoning reverence   (5) glorious accomplishment

26. NEFARIOUS — (1) terrific   (2) wandering   (3) sporadic   (4) motley   (5) wicked

27. QUACKERY — (1) charlatanism   (2) raucous noise   (3) rambunctiousness   (4) desuetude   (5) insolence

28. RECANT — (1) sing again   (2) repudiate   (3) reaffirm   (4) novel   (5) paraphrase

29. TRANSGRESS — (1) cross over   (2) interpret   (3) sin   (4) wander   (5) retreat

30. JUDICIOUS — (1) forensic   (2) prudent   (3) pertaining to a judge   (4) executive   (5) formidable

APTITUDE TEST FOUR

PART *A* — SYNONYMS AND ANTONYMS

Time: 30 Minutes

I. *Directions:* In each group below, you will find words and phrases numbered (1) to (5). Choose the word or expression that is most nearly *similar* in meaning to the capitalized word.

1. TANTAMOUNT — (1) more than enough   (2) equal   (3) a little less than   (4) superior to   (5) transcending

2. SALLY — (1) to leap forth   (2) to retreat   (3) to walk slowly   (4) to respond   (5) to jut out

3. HOMILY — (1) denunciation   (2) ugly   (3) sermon   (4) masculine   (5) religious

4. FESTOON — (1) to generate pus   (2) festival   (3) object of special devotion   (4) mural painting   (5) garland

5. WILY — (1) voluntary   (2) cruel   (3) despotic   (4) crafty   (5) misanthropic

6. TENET — (1) doctrine   (2) receptacle   (3) grasp   (4) a holding   (5) heresy

7. RECIPROCAL — (1) receptive   (2) mutual   (3) captive   (4) unacceptable   (5) laudatory

8. INSCRUTABLE — (1) rigid   (2) irrevocable   (3) inveterate   (4) inhospitable   (5) incomprehensible

9. ACCRUE — (1) accede   (2) acclaim   (3) yellow   (4) count as an addition or increase   (5) cause to assemble

10. COTERIE — (1) cabal   (2) existing at the same time   (3) group of persons   (4) coeval   (5) blood relationship

11. CRUCIAL — (1) increasing   (2) decisive   (3) crushing   (4) sad   (5) sacrificing

12. FLAUNT — (1) to display boastfully   (2) to disobey   (3) to blemish   (4) to violate   (5) to show cowardice

13. IMMOLATE — (1) to inflict   (2) to violate   (3) to sacrifice   (4) to soften   (5) to inspire

APTITUDE TEST FOUR

14. QUAIL — (1) to construct   (2) to dig   (3) to rebuke   (4) to cower   (5) to slash

15. UBIQUITOUS — (1) vulgar   (2) existing everywhere   (3) almighty   (4) inquiring   (5) fantastic

16. VIE — (1) life   (2) to examine closely   (3) unholy   (4) to strive for superiority   (5) to view

17. APPRISE — (1) to inform   (2) to draw near   (3) to inflate   (4) to deflate   (5) to anticipate

18. WHEEDLE — (1) to circumscribe   (2) to cringe   (3) to coax   (4) to insinuate   (5) to amuse

19. GRIMACE — (1) facial distortion   (2) to depress   (3) to utter   (4) to brandish   (5) a jest

20. METTLE — (1) substance   (2) resentment   (3) cowardice   (4) courtesy   (5) quality of temperament

21. OBVIATE — (1) to make obvious   (2) to make obsolete   (3) to observe   (4) to render unnecessary   (5) to deny

22. LONGEVITY — (1) length of life   (2) extensiveness   (3) state of longing   (4) relating to length   (5) antiquity

23. GUILE — (1) part of an ocean   (2) deceit   (3) sea bird   (4) musical instrument   (4) German coin

24. ACOUSTICS — (1) lack of hearing   (2) crescendo   (3) science of sound   (4) science of language   (5) gymnastics

25. ASKANCE — (1) request   (2) turned to one side   (3) stupidly   (4) aspect   (5) with distrust

26. DROSS — (1) waste-matter   (2) gold   (3) long spell of dry weather   (4) hard work   (5) a drum

27. VICARIOUS — (1) religious   (2) vicious   (3) pertaining to food   (4) acting for another   (5) seriously ill

28. JARGON — (1) happy   (2) idle talk   (3) unintelligible language   (4) translation   (5) foreign language

29. LINEAMENT — (1) facial outlines   (2) line-up   (3) linkage   (4) fine linen   (5) family background

30. ANTITHESIS — (1) remedy   (2) chemical   (3) old age   (4) substance opposing decay   (5) contrast of ideas

COLLEGE ENTRANCE TESTS

II. *Directions:* In each group below, you will find a capitalized word followed by five words or expressions numbered (1) to (5). Choose the word or expression that is most nearly *opposite* in meaning to the capitalized word.

1. MUNDANE — (1) corporeal (2) spiritual (3) liberal (4) contemporary (5) affluent

2. INSUPERABLE — (1) redoubtable (2) invidious (3) gainly (4) retentive (5) vulnerable

3. DISCURSIVE — (1) cursory (2) answering (3) digress (4) terse (5) penurious

4. GAUCHE — (1) ungainly (2) sinister (3) corrupt (4) deft (5) perfunctory

5. EMINENT — (1) nonentity (2) restrictive (3) luminary (4) backward (5) diffident

6. EULOGIZE — (1) revive (2) aggravate (3) elicit (4) capitulate (5) asperse

7. ITINERANT — (1) settled (2) repetitious (3) traditional (4) surreptitious (5) hostile

8. AMALGAMATE — (1) abrogate (2) indict (3) sunder (4) accrue (5) absolve

9. GAINSAY — (1) self-evident (2) acquit (3) retreat (4) render profitless (5) substantiate

10. URBANE — (1) dulcet (2) emollient (3) boorish (4) stupid (5) cosmopolitan

11. REFRACTORY — (1) obdurate (2) obnoxious (3) amenable (4) mild (5) careful

12. ANTAGONIST — (1) paragon (2) confederate (3) garrulous (4) culpable (5) pugnacious

13. SUPERCILIOUS — (1) ignominious (2) finical (3) opprobrious (4) obsequious (5) opulent

14. GULLIBLE — (1) petulant (2) skeptical (3) incredible (4) credulous (5) illiterate

15. ARID — (1) primeval (2) precarious (3) fertile (4) lavish (5) lurid

16. OBTUSE — (1) ponderous (2) blunt (3) limpid (4) acute (5) opposite

APTITUDE TEST FOUR

17. SOVEREIGN — (1) dependent   (2) proletariat   (3) saturnine   (4) sire   (5) highest

18. AVERSION — (1) repugnance   (2) parsimony   (3) craving   (4) lack of enjoyment   (5) predilection

19. TERSE — (1) succinct   (2) verbose   (3) pithy   (4) pleasant   (5) unattractive

20. BENISON — (1) benignity   (2) blessing   (3) malevolence   (4) beneficence   (5) malediction

21. PACIFISM — (1) serenity   (2) military force   (3) bellicosity   (4) worry   (5) opposition to an armistice

22. CANTANKEROUS — (1) plebeian   (2) ill-natured   (3) petulant   (4) even-tempered   (5) stationary

23. FLORID — (1) ruddy   (2) pallid   (3) quixotic   (4) ostentatious   (5) moving slowly

24. CAPRICIOUS — (1) governed by fickleness   (2) resisting capture   (3) playfulness   (4) constant   (5) refusing to agree

25. OVERT — (1) clandestine   (2) patent   (3) overturned   (4) manifest   (5) undefeated

26. COMPATIBLE — (1) obtrusive   (2) despotic   (3) depleted   (4) non-competitive   (5) incongruous

27. DOLEFUL — (1) dispassionate   (2) convivial   (3) without aroma   (4) consecrated   (5) remiss

28. IMPENITENT — (1) patient   (2) depraved   (3) contrite   (4) consolable   (5) disconsolate

29. RENEGADE — (1) reticent   (2) affirmative   (3) apostate   (4) disciple   (5) dissolute

30. DEFUNCT — (1) extant   (2) duplicity   (3) defiant   (4) imperious   (5) inflated

PART *B* — ANALOGIES

Time: 30 Minutes

Directions: In each group below, you will find two capitalized words which bear a certain logical relationship to each other. These are followed by five pairs of words numbered (1) to (5). Choose the pair of words which have the same relationship to each other as do the capitalized words.

1. BUMPTIOUS : CONCEITED : : (1) affluent : smug (2) cynical: self-assertive (3) refractory : opinionated (4) diffident : modest (5) altruistic : egocentric

2. FACADE : BUILDING : : (1) exterior : surface (2) veneer : furniture (3) feature : countenance (4) army : vanguard (5) proscenium : stage

3. JEALOUSY : GREEN : : (1) royalty : carmine (2) ire : azure (3) rage : crimson (4) purity : iridescent (5) avarice : purple

4. CONDUIT : WATER : : (1) vein : blood (2) trench : mire (3) roadway : land (4) funnel : liquid (5) canal : traffic

5. TOGA : SUIT : : (1) archaic : obsolete (2) nefarious : modern (3) obscure : novel (4) antediluvian : superannuated (5) extinct : extant

6. ROAR : HUM : : (1) purr : buzz (2) bang : clang (3) reverberate : echo (4) clangor : tinkle (5) peal : boom

7. CODE : MESSAGE : : (1) charade : idea (2) masquerade : truth (3) pseudonym : writings (4) identity : incognito (5) ambush : escape

8. THRESHOLD : ROOM : : (1) coast : continent (2) lintel : door (3) quay : wharf (4) border : country (5) fringe : skirt

9. TRILOGY : QUARTO : : (1) trisect : cleave (2) treble : quadruple (3) triad : myriad (4) ramification : cleavage (5) triangle : polygon

10. BEREAVEMENT : LAMENT : : (1) birth : exult (2) disappointment : disdain (3) fortune : rue (4) loss : disparage (5) death : expiate

11. SLOTH : INERTIA : : (1) vacillation : quiescence (2) obstinacy : irresolution (3) torpor : inactivity (4) languor : abeyance (5) industry : stimulation

12. ACQUITTAL : RELEASE : : (1) exoneration : incarceration (2) arraignment : indictment (3) franchise : penalty (4) redress : dismissal (5) conviction : impeachment

13. ELLIPSE : CIRCLE : : (1) expand : contract (2) convex : concave (3) diamond : square (4) hollow : cube (5) orange : spiral

14. REBUFF : ACQUIESCE : : (1) spurn : spur (2) snub : consent (3) repudiate : repulse (4) concur : dissent (5) knuckle : cater

15. MOTTLED : SPOTS : : (1) streaked : lines (2) variegated : kinds (3) kaleidoscopic : colors (4) concentric : centers (5) dappled : blemishes

16. JEST : DEPRESSION : : (1) wit : pleasantry (2) humor : panacea (3) variety : monotony (4) opiate : illness (5) nostrum : folly

17. IMPROPRIETY : DECORUM : : (1) remorse : guilt (2) compunction : remorse (3) invulnerability : attack (4) intrepidity : cowardice (5) apprehension : fear

18. AFFLICTED : CURE : : (1) transgressor : justice (2) drydock : ship (3) grief : solace (4) alias : anonymity (5) refugee : asylum

19. LOW : MOO : : (1) bleat : shriek (2) hoot : mew (3) simper : guffaw (4) chirp : cackle (5) yelp : bay

20. APIARY : BEE : : (1) aviary : bird (2) manger : cattle (3) eskimo : igloo (4) cloister : religion (5) fold : horse

21. STUDY : UNDERSTANDING : : (1) assiduity : knowledge (2) achievement : perfection (3) industry : virtuoso (4) repetition : skill (5) practice : mastery

22. CONFORM : ORTHODOX : : (1) deviate : heterodox (2) misbelieve : paradox (3) dissent : radical (4) procrastinate : cynical (5) scoff : critical

23. ECONOMY : PARSIMONY : : (1) indigence : poverty (2) destitution : avarice (3) spending : prodigality (4) avarice : lavishness (5) penny-wise : pound-foolish

24. BIBLIOPHILE : BOOK : : (1) ecclesiastic : ideas (2) chauvinist : traditions (3) martinet : war (4) philatelist : stamps (5) numismatist : antiques

25. GENESIS : CONSUMMATION : : (1) prologue : plot (2) inception : terminus (3) debut : exodus (4) portal : vestibule (5) embryo : egg

26. SCINTILLA : BULK : : (1) tinge : tint (2) trace : vestige (3) particle : mote (4) titanic : stupendous (5) mannequin : mammoth

27. MERCURY : VOLATILE : : (1) chromium : decorative (2) nitrogen : gaseous (3) aluminum : light (4) glass : brittle (5) dacron : sleazy

28. INFREQUENTLY : INCESSANTLY : : (1) seldom : sporadically (2) rarely : constantly (3) oft : ne'er (4) ever : never (5) hardly : nonetheless

29. KILOMETER : ROD : : (1) avoirdupois : metric (2) ounce : gram (3) kilogram : meter (4) centimeter : inch (5) cubic : linear

30. ALLEGE : PROVE : : (1) fabricate : confirm (2) evasion : sham (3) charge : convict (4) aver : affirm (5) feign : simulate

PART *C*

Time: 30 Minutes

I. Comprehension

Directions: In each selection below, you will find one or more blanks indicating the omission of a word, or a phrase, or a pair of words or phrases which will make the sense complete. Following the selection are five choices numbered (1) to (5). Choose the item that you think will best complete the meaning of the selection.

1. A statement that is deliberately .... with intention to deceive may be said to be ....

(1) vague — hypocritical (2) forthright — exceptionable (3) ambiguous — equivocal (4) specious — forthright (5) emphatic — devious

2. One quality that is a definite handicap is the author's prose style, which vacillates between a rather .... style and a penchant for excessively .... passages.

(1) ornate — florid (2) prosaic — florid (3) petulant — irritating (4) florid — flamboyant (5) prosaic — raucous

3. American science and engineering possess .... strength and vigor; and if we proceed .... and decisively we can maintain them in the flourishing state required by our national welfare and security.

(1) faltering — assiduously (2) prodigal — tentatively (3) potential — circumspectly (4) unfathomable — warily (5) prodigious — diligently

APTITUDE TEST FOUR

4. A .... is one who pretends to knowledge and ability.

    (1) hypocrite   (2) hoax   (3) novice   (4) charlatan   (5) paragon

5. It is both .... and terrifying to view the wreckage of great civilizations. Here in the Cambodian jungles, largely obscured by foliage, lie miles of ruins, the pompous shards of Angkor. Angkor was the seat of that boastful Khmer Empire, which in its day claimed to be ....

    (1) amusing — omnipresent   (2) somber — omnipotent   (3) dolorous — mutable   (4) incredible — immaculate   (5) dolorous — vulnerable

6. A .... person is seldom ....

    (1) saturnine — morose   (2) sagacious — perspicacious   (3) procrastinating — deferential   (4) vacillating — vicarious   (5) supine — redoubtable

7. During the last decade of the sixteenth century, politics at the court of Queen Elizabeth were dominated by the disruptive personality of Robert Devereux, second Earl of Essex. Brilliant, compelling, ... popularity and praise, he concealed an hysterical streak which drove him on to a seemingly inevitable doom. His career and his retinue depended upon the force of his glittering and unstable personality, ..., in spite of the age and the nobility of his family, he was not endowed with opulence or wide estates. Although some of his supporters were tenants of the Devereux's, and some were his liveried retainers, most were bound to him by the attraction of his person and the knowledge that he stood high in Elizabeth's favor.

    (1) devoid of — hence   (2) magnanimous — consequently   (3) avid for — for   (4) craving for — subsequently   (5) cowering — thus

8. When all his limitations have been noted, the achievement of Herodotus as a historian nevertheless remains impressive. Very few Greek and Roman historians were so .... in collecting their material. His sources were of varying value; but most of them were remarkably good. His description of Persian organization is based on Persian records. His successors could add little to his account of Athenian history in the sixth century. He grasped the main essence of Spartan institutions. Herodotus in his history reached the .... of historical narration.

    (1) perfunctory — nadir   (2) meretricious — abyss   (3) capricious — apex   (4) momentous — impasse   (5) meticulous — pinnacle

9. A person who is .... in the face of danger is a(n) ....

(1) valiant — hedonist   (2) imperturbable — stoic   (3) implacable — zealot   (4) sarcastic — satirist   (5) inconstant — epicurean

10. A(n) .... foe can seldom be............ ....

(1) irretrievable — conquered   (2) irreconcilable — aroused   (3) implacable — appeased   (4) craven — recalcitrant   (5) docile — compromised

11. It was basic research, carried out by seekers after knowledge for its own sake, that gave us all the products of our highly advanced technological civilization. It was basic research that gave us the electron, the basis of the multi-billion-dollar electronics industry; the knowledge of the existence of electromagnetic waves, which made possible radio, television, radar, and many other modern marvels; the discovery of the nucleus of the atom, which opened the way to the Atomic Age. Similarly, it was basic **research that gave us penicillin and the antibiotics that led to the under**standing of the underlying causes of the infectious diseases. And upon basic research rest our hopes for the conquest of cancer, heart disease, and the degenerative diseases that .... our lives at their most productive period. Yet, so little is the importance of basic research understood that a former Secretary of Defense could remark .... that "basic research is when you don't know what you are doing."

(1) protract — impartially   (2) curtail — disparagingly   (3) brighten — naively   (4) shorten — eloquently   (5) distract — offensively

12. Joan Nicholas, who made her Metropolitan Opera debut this season, is a soprano with a mind as well as a voice. The combination is not ....; seldom has a soprano appeared in recent times bearing these .... qualities in such a harmony.

(1) commonplace — preeminent   (2) novel — egregious   (3) compatible — inherent   (4) auspicious — incongruous   (5) harmonious — disparate

13. Those who appeal to the .... in people to arouse discontent for the purpose of advancing their own political ends may be termed ....

(1) vulgarity – autocrats (2) baseness – fascists (3) aesthetic – raconteurs (4) bias – demagogues (5) gullibility – bigots

14. Attila, the son of Mundzuk, deduced his noble, perhaps his regal descent from the ancient Huns, who had formerly contended with the monarchs of China. His features, according to the observation of a Gothic historian, bore the stamp of his national origin; and the portrait of Attila exhibits the genuine deformity of a modern Calmuck; a large head, a swarthy complexion, small deep-seated eyes, a flat nose, a few hairs in the place of a beard, broad shoulders, and a short square body, of nervous strength, though of a disproportioned form. The .... step and demeanour of the King of the Huns expressed the consciousness of his superiority above the rest of mankind; and he had a custom of rolling his eyes, as if he wished to enjoy the terror which he inspired. Yet this savage hero was not inaccessible to pity: his .... enemies might realistically quell their fears in the hope of peace or pardon; and Attila was considered by his subjects as a just and indulgent master.

(1) haughty — suppliant (2) meek — haughty (3) halting — cringing (4) supercilious — inveterate (5) cantankerous — querulous

15. The difference in the use of words by different writers is as great as that in the use of paints by great and poor artists; and there is as great a difference in the effect upon the understanding and the sensibilities of their readers. Who that is familiar with Bacon's writings can ever fail to recognize one of his sentences, so .... and concise, and going to the mark as if from a gun? In Bacon, it has been remarked, language was always the flexible and obedient instrument of the thought; not, as in the productions of a lower order of mind, its rebellious and .... slave.

(1) verbose — refractory (2) diffuse — obsequious (3) terse — flexible (4) pithy — recalcitrant (5) captious — amenable

II. Synonyms and Antonyms

Directions: In each group below, you will find words numbered (1) to (5). Select the two words in the group that are most nearly *similar or opposite* to each other in meaning.

1. (1) profuse (2) recondite (3) synthetic (4) abstruse (5) perspicuous

2. (1) irate (2) indigenous (3) indigent (4) ornate (5) destitute

3. (1) spurious (2) irascible (3) surreptitious (4) authentic (5) recalcitrant

4. (1) retrieve (2) coy (3) accede (4) demur (5) capitulate

5. (1) express (2) articulate (3) stipulate (4) gesticulate (5) banter

6. (1) academic (2) pedantic (3) theoretical (4) abstemious (5) valedictory

7. (1) impale (2) extirpate (3) expound (4) spurn (5) rear

8. (1) Nordic (2) germane (3) impertinent (4) extrinsic (5) pertinacious

9. (1) chimerical (2) meandering (3) recrudescent (4) insurgent (5) rebellious

10. (1) receptive (2) reciprocal (3) taciturn (4) ignominious (5) mutual

11. (1) wistful (2) pensive (3) ponderous (4) recriminatory (5) literary

12. (1) incredible (2) impalpable (3) inert (4) tangible (5) turgid

13. (1) consoling (2) slothful (3) redolent (4) perambulatory (5) aromatic

14. (1) palliate (2) ingratiate (3) solicit (4) exile (5) mitigate

15. (1) satellite (2) novice (3) lackey (4) brilliant light (5) ancient

16. (1) reticent (2) mirthful (3) lugubrious (4) lax (5) unwieldy

17. (1) stark (2) wroth (3) lethargic (4) ornate (5) insane

18. (1) disavow (2) censure (3) purge (4) ostracize (5) expurgate

19. (1) wary (2) circumscribed (3) rash (4) epigrammatic (5) lucid

20. (1) prosaic (2) baneful (3) concise (4) commonplace (5) literal

APTITUDE TEST FOUR

21. (1) desecrated (2) desultory (3) sanctimonious (4) sacrosanct (5) methodical

22. (1) deviate (2) venerable (3) remunerative (4) heterodox (5) paradoxical

23. (1) indiscreet (2) judicious (3) orderly (4) perfervid (5) discrete

24. (1) teem (2) abound (3) condone (4) associate (5) leap

25. (1) mercenary (2) remit (3) sedulous (4) perfunctory (5) paltry

26. (1) laud (2) admonish (3) expiate (4) pervert (5) allude

27. (1) sarcastic (2) didactic (3) instructional (4) strategic (5) satirical

28. (1) expedient (2) parsimonious (3) munificent (4) mendicant (5) mendacious

29. (1) derogatory (2) arrogant (3) moot (4) disparaging (5) equivocal

30. (1) avaricious (2) recreant (3) intrepid (4) costly (5) apocryphal

VOCABULARY
SCHOLARSHIP
TESTS

Directions: In each group below, you will find one *italicized* word followed by five words or phrases numbered (1) to (5). In each case choose the word or phrase that has most nearly the same meaning as the italicized word.

TEST ONE

1. *cumulative* —(1) additive (2) clumsy (3) cumbersome (4) incorrect (5) secretive
2. *epigram* — (1) chemical term (2) exclamation (3) outer skin (4) pithy saying (5) tombstone
3. *gesticulate* — (1) dance (2) digest easily (3) ridicule (4) travel (5) use gestures
4. *beguile* — (1) benefit (2) bind (3) deceive (4) envy (5) petition
5. *avid* — (1) eager (2) glowing (3) indifferent (4) lax (5) potent
6. *labyrinth* — (1) laboratory (2) maze (3) path (4) portal (5) room
7. *regurgitate* — (1) make new investments (2) obliterate (3) restore to solvency (4) slacken (5) cast or pour back
8. *podium* — (1) chemical element (2) dais (3) foot specialist (4) magistrate (5) Roman infantryman
9. *bereft* — (1) annoyed (2) awarded (3) deprived (4) enraged (5) insane
10. *elucidate* — (1) condense (2) escape (3) evade (4) explain (5) shine through
11. *emollient* — (1) comical (2) despicable (3) enthusiastic (4) raucous (5) tending to soften or soothe
12. *nostalgic* — (1) expressive (2) forgetful (3) homesick (4) inconstant (5) seasick
13. *expiate* — (1) atone for (2) die (3) hasten (4) imitate (5) make holy
14. *paradox* — (1) accepted opinion (2) axiom (3) contradiction (4) enigma (5) pattern
15. *archetype* — (1) bowman (2) original model (3) public records (4) roguishness (5) star
16. *mundane* — (1) deformed (2) free (3) rough-shelled (4) tearful (5) worldly
17. *palliative*—(1) boring (2) callous (3) permanent (4) rendering less severe (5) unyielding
18. *foment* –(1) curb (2) explode (3) rouse (4) turn into wine (5) undermine

TEST ONE

19. *predacious* — (1) beautiful (2) incongruous (3) peaceful (4) preying (5) valuable

20. *stark* — (1) absent-minded (2) bristling (3) sheer (4) involuntary (5) shining

21. *blatant* — (1) clamorous (2) conceited (3) prudish (4) reticent (5) unsuited

22. *adversity* — (1) advertising (2) counsel (3) criticism (4) misfortune (5) proficiency

23. *cadaverous* — (1) cheerful (2) contemptible (3) like a corpse (4) hungry (5) ill-bred

24. *wraith* — (1) anger (2) apparition (3) figurine (4) mannequin (5) model

25. *perspicacity* — (1) intensity (2) dullness (3) keenness (4) vastness (5) wideness

26. *extraneous* — (1) derived (2) external (3) unsuitable (4) visible (5) wasteful

27. *paroxysm*—(1) catastrophe (2) convulsion (3) illusion (4) lack of harmony (5) loss of all bodily movement

28. *sapient* — (1) sage (2) foolish (3) mocking (4) soapy (5) youthful

29. *flaccid* — (1) flabby (2) golden (3) hard (4) powerful (5) well-educated

30. *impecunious* — (1) frugal (2) guiltless (3) miserly (4) relating to money (5) poor

31. *spurious* — (1) concise (2) false (3) obstinate (4) sarcastic (5) severe

32. *subservient* — (1) existing (2) obsequious (3) related (4) profound (5) useful

33. *importune* — (1) aggrandize (2) carry (3) exaggerate (4) prolong (5) urge

34. *indigenous* — (1) confused (2) native (3) poor (4) unconcerned (5) wrathful

35. *uncouth* — (1) ugly (2) inviolate (3) holy (4) instrumental (5) unmannerly

TEST TWO

1. *disparage* — (1) belittle (2) degrade (3) erase (4) reform (5) scatter
2. *limpid* — (1) calm (2) clear (3) crippled (4) delightful (5) opaque
3. *derisive* — (1) dividing (2) furnishing (3) reflecting (4) expressing ridicule (5) suggesting
4. *debilitate* — (1) encourage (2) insinuate (3) prepare (4) turn away (5) weaken
5. *opulent* — (1) fearful (2) free (3) oversized (4) trustful (5) wealthy
6. *blandishment* — (1) dislike (2) flattery (3) ostentation (4) praise (5) rejection
7. *cryptic* — (1) appealing (2) arched (3) deathly (4) hidden (5) intricate
8. *raucous* — (1) harsh (2) loud (3) querulous (4) rational 5) violent
9. *avidity* — (1) friendliness (2) greediness (3) resentment (4) speed (5) thirst
10. *epitome* — (1) conclusion (2) effort (3) letter (4) summary (5) summit
11. *hiatus* — (1) branch (2) disease (3) gaiety (4) insect (5) opening
12. *plenary* — (1) easy (2) empty (3) full (4) rewarding (5) untrustworthy
13. *capricious* — (1) active (2) fickle (3) opposed (4) sheeplike (5) slippery
14. *specious* — (1) frank (2) particular (3) plausible (4) suspicious (5) vigorous
15. *extirpate* — (1) besmirch (2) clean (3) eradicate (4) favor (5) subdivide
16. *equivocal* — (1) doubtful (2) medium (3) monotonous (4) musical (5) well-balanced
17. *benison* — (1) approval (2) blessing (3) gift (4) prayer (5) reward
18. *beatific* — (1) giving bliss (2) eager (3) hesitant (4) lovely (5) sad
19. *sanguine* — (1) limp (2) mechanical (3) muddy (4) red (5) stealthy
20. *surcease* — (1) end (2) hope (3) resignation (4) sleep (5) sweetness
21. *sentient* — (1) very emotional (2) capable of feeling (3) hostile (4) sympathetic (5) wise
22. *obviate* — (1) grasp (2) reform (3) simplify (4) smooth (5) make unnecessary
23. *peruse* — (1) endure (2) perpetuate (3) read (4) undertake (5) urge

TEST TWO

24. *rancor* — (1) dignity   (2) fierceness   (3) odor   (4) spite   (5) suspicion

25. *truncheon* — (1) baton   (2) canopy   (3) dish   (4) gun   (5) rejected food

26. *sebaceous* — (1) fatty   (2) fluid   (3) porous   (4) transparent   (5) watery

27. *dilatory* — (1) hairy   (2) happy-go-lucky   (3) ruined   (4) tardy   (5) well-to-do

28. *ebullition* — (1) bathing   (2) boiling   (3) refilling   (4) retiring   (5) returning

29. *relegate* — (1) banish   (2) deprive   (3) designate   (4) report   (5) request

30. *recondite* — (1) brittle   (2) profound   (3) explored-   (4) exposed   (5) uninformed

31. *redolent* — (1) odorous   (2) quick   (3) refined   (4) repulsive   (5) supple

32. *dissimulate* — (1) confound   (2) pretend   (3) question   (4) separate   (5) strain

33. *sublime* — (1) below par   (2) highly praised   (3) extreme   (4) noble   (5) settled

34. *termagant* — (1) fever   (2) noisy woman   (3) sea bird   (4) sedative   (5) squirrel

35. *sedulous* — (1) deceptive   (2) diligent   (3) grassy   (4) hateful   (5) sweet

36. *vitiate* — (1) contaminate   (2) flavor   (3) freshen   (4) illuminate   (5) refer

37. *curvet* —- (1) come around   (2) follow   (3) leap   (4) restrain   (5) warp

38. *adventitious* – (1) accidental   (2) courageous   (3) favorable   (4) risk taking   (5) unexpected

39. *animus* — (1) animosity   (2) breath   (3) faith   (4) light   (5) poison

40. *descried*—(1) hailed   (2) rebuffed   (3) recalled   (4) regretted   (5) sighted

TEST THREE

1. *adulation* — (1) approach   (2) echo (3) flattery   (4) gift   (5) imi-. tation
2. *subsequently* — (1) continually   (2) factually   (3) accordingly   (4) incidentally   (5) later
3. *expurgate* — (1) amplify   (2) emphasize   (3) offend   (4) purify   (5) renew
4. *liaison* — (1) derivative   (2) liability   (3) link   (4) malice   (5) officer
5. *sedentary* — (1) careful   (2) inactive   (3) notched   (4) pleasant   (5) uneventful
6. *lassitude* — (1) childishness   (2) energy   (3) ignorance   (4) languor   (5) seriousness
7. *altruistically* — (1) egotistically   (2) harmfully   (3) harshly   (4) highly   (5) unselfishly
8. *perfidious* — (1) ambiguous   (2) flawless   (3) perforated   (4) treacherous   (5) trusting
9. *consummate* — (1) achieve   (2) devour   (3) effuse   (4) ignite   (5) take
10. *munificently*—(1) acutely   (2) awkwardly   (3) cruelly   (4) generously   (5) militarily
11. *lugubrious* — (1) calm   (2) doleful   (3) tepid   (4) wan   (5) warm
12. *apathetic* — (1) desolate   (2) emotional   (3) incorrigible   (4) passive   (5) sad
13. *coterie* — (1) clique   (2) cure-all   (3) expert judge   (4) forerunner   (5) society girl
14. *conduit* — (1) doorway   (2) electric generator   (3) power   (4) screen   (5) tube
15. *shibboleth* — (1) friend in need   (2) lonely home   (3) personal complaint   (4) reason for action   (5) watchword
16. *evanescent* — (1) colorful   (2) consecrated   (3) converted   (4) empty   (5) vanishing
17. *parsimonious* — (1) cautious   (2) ecclesiastical   (3) luxurious   (4) stingy   (5) unique
18. *Machiavellian* — (1) cunning   (2) humble   (3) kingly   (4) machine-like   (5) saintly
19. *compendium* — (1) amplification   (2) appendix   (3) expansion   (4) paraphrase   (5) summary
20. *megalomania* — (1) desire for beauty   (2) mania for sympathy   (3) miserliness   (4) passion for grandness   (5) pity for the poor
21. *torpor* — (1) cyclone   (2) frenzy   (3) sluggishness   (4) strain   (5) twisting

22. *esoteric* — (1) clear   (2) external   (3) popular   (4) secret   (5) uncertain

23. *superciliously* — (1) critically   (2) disdainfully   (3) hypersensitively   (4) naively   (5) softly

24. *abstemious* — (1) blatant   (2) exhilarating   (3) greedy   (4) temperate   (5) wasteful

25. *ken* — (1) acceptance   (2) belief   (3) dune   (4) knowledge   (5) woody glen

26. *germane* — (1) diseased   (2) foreign   (3) infected   (4) pertinent   (5) polished

27. *vituperation* — (1) abuse   (2) appendectomy   (3) complication   (4) rejuvenation   (5) repeal

28. *chimerical* — (1) clever   (2) delusive   (3) experimental   (4) foreign   (5) provisional

29. *dulcimer* — (1) dolly   (2) doublet   (3) duenna   (4) gadget   (5) musical instrument

30. *sartorial* — (1) disheveled   (2) frozen   (3) satirical   (4) tailored   (5) warm

31. *vertigo* — (1) curiosity   (2) dizziness   (3) enlivenment   (4) greenness   (5) invigoration

32. *debacle* — (1) ceremony   (2) collapse   (3) dance   (4) deficit   (5) dispute

33. *condign* — (1) deserved   (2) hidden   (3) perplexed   (4) pretended   (5) unworthy

34. *ephemerally* — (1) enduringly   (2) lightly   (3) openly   (4) suspiciously   (5) transiently

35. *histrionic* — (1) authentic   (2) hysterical   (3) reportorial   (4) sibilant   (5) theatrical

36. *urbanity* — (1) aggressiveness   (2) mercenary   (3) municipal   (4) rustic   (5) suavity

37. *truculent* — (1) rambling   (2) relenting   (3) savage   (4) tranquil   (5) weary

38. *inveigh* — (1) allure   (2) entice   (3) guide cautiously   (4) originate   (5) speak bitterly

39. *desultory* — (1) delaying   (2) disconnected   (3) flagrant   (4) insulting   (5) irritating

40. *ingenuous*—(1) clever   (2) frank   (3) ignorant   (4) native   (5) unkind

MASTERY
VOCABULARY
TESTS

Directions: In each group below, you will find one *italicized* word followed by five words or phrases numbered (1) to (5). In each case choose the word or phrase that has most nearly the same meaning as the italicized word.

TEST ONE

1. *laud* — (1) praise   (2) cleanse   (3) replace   (4) squander   (5) frown upon
2. *taunt* — (1) jeer at   (2) tighten   (3) rescue   (4) interest   (5) ward off
3. *deity* — (1) renown   (2) divinity   (3) delicacy   (4) destiny   (5) futility
4. *gravity* — (1) displeasure   (2) thankfulness   (3) suffering   (4) roughness   (5) seriousness
5. *contemptuous* — (1) thoughtful   (2) soiled   (3) dishonorable   (4) scornful   (5) self-satisfied
6. *waive* — (1) exercise   (2) swing   (3) claim   (4) give up   (5) wear out
7. *aspire* — (1) fade away   (2) excite   (3) desire earnestly   (4) breathe heavily   (5) roughen
8. *pertinent* — (1) related   (2) saucy   (3) quick   (4) impatient   (5) excited
9. *devastation*—(1) desolation   (2) displeasure   (3) dishonor   (4) neglect   (5) religious fervor
10. *imminent* — (1) sudden   (2) important   (3) delayed   (4) threatening   (5) forceful

TEST TWO

1. *infiltrate* — (1) pass through   (2) stop   (3) consider   (4) challenge openly   (5) meet secretly
2. *revocation* — (1) certificate   (2) repeal   (3) animation   (4) license   (5) plea
3. *loquacious* — (1) grim   (2) stern   (3) talkative   (4) lighthearted   (5) liberty-loving
4. *aperture* — (1) basement   (2) opening   (3) phantom   (4) protective coloring   (5) light refreshment
5. *pungent* — (1) biting   (2) smooth   (3) quarrelsome   (4) wrong   (5) proud
6. *corroborate* — (1) deny   (2) elaborate   (3) confirm   (4) gnaw   (5) state
7. *benevolence* — (1) good fortune   (2) well-being   (3) inheritance   (4) violence   (5) charitableness
8. *petulant* — (1) rotten   (2) fretful   (3) unrelated   (4) weird   (5) throbbing

9. *derelict* — (1) abandoned   (2) widowed   (3) faithful   (4) insincere   (5) hysterical
10. *incisive* — (1) stimulating   (2) accidental   (3) brief   (4) penetrating   (5) final

TEST THREE

1. *sulk* — (1) cry   (2) annoy   (3) lament   (4) be sullen   (5) scorn
2. *flounder* — (1) investigate   (2) label   (3) struggle   (4) consent   (5) escape
3. *parley* — (1) discussion   (2) thoroughfare   (3) salon   (4) surrender   (5) division
4. *maestro* — (1) official   (2) ancestor   (3) teacher   4) guard   (5) alien
5. *meandering* — (1) cruel   (2) adjusting   (3) winding   (4) smooth   (5) combining
6. *gnarled* — (1) angry   (2) bitter   (3) twisted   (4) ancient   (5) embroidered
7. *temperance* — (1) moderation   (2) climate   (3) carelessness   (4) disagreeableness   (5) rigidity
8. *precarious* — (1) foresighted   (2) careful   (3) modest   (4) headstrong   (5) uncertain
9. *covetous* — (1) undisciplined   (2) grasping   (3) timid   (4) insincere   (5) secretive
10. *privation* — (1) reward   (2) superiority in rank   (3) hardship   (4) suitability of behavior   (5) solitude

TEST FOUR

1. *reluctant* — (1) displeased   (2) stern   (3) conclusive   (4) voluntary   (5) unwilling
2. *wary* — (1) dangerous   (2) cautious   (3) clear   (4) warm   (5) exciting
3. *interloper* — (1) alien   (2) intruder   (3) questioner   (4) magician   (5) rainmaker
4. *inconsistent* — (1) insane   (2) senatorial   (3) undeviating   (4) contradictory   (5) faithful
5 *vulnerable* — (1) usually harmless   (2) slyly greedy   (3) poisonous   (4) deeply religious   (5) open to attack
6. *indignation* — (1) poverty   (2) anger   (3) exaggeration   (4) mercy   (5) publicity
7. *abate* — (1) strike out   (2) catch   (3) diminish   (4) embarrass   (5) wound
8. *sustenance* — (1) nourishment   (2) overabundance   (3) anxiety   (4) equality   (5) alertness

9. *bulwark* — (1) target (2) grass (3) safeguard (4) tail (5) compartment
10. *demeanor* — (1) bearing (2) expenditure (3) irritability (4) questionnaire (5) death

TEST FIVE

1. *bondage* — (1) poverty (2) redemption (3) slavery (4) retirement (5) complaint
2. *agility* — (1) wisdom (2) nimbleness (3) agreeableness (4) simplicity (5) excitement
3. *abdicate* — (1) achieve (2) protest (3) renounce (4) demand (5) steal
4. *stifle* — (1) talk nonsense (2) sidestep (3) depress (4) smother (5) stick
5. *edict* — (1) abbreviation (2) lie (3) carbon copy (4) correction (5) decree
6. *amity* — (1) ill will (2) hope (3) pity (4) friendship (5) pleasure
7. *coercion* — (1) force (2) disgust (3) suspicion (4) pleasure (5) criticism
8. *abash* — (1) embarrass (2) encourage (3) punish (4) surrender (5) overthrow
9. *taciturn* — (1) weak (2) evil (3) tender (4) silent (5) sensitive
10. *remiss* — (1) memorable (2) neglectful (3) useless (4) prompt (5) exact

TEST SIX

1. *dubious* — (1) economical (2) well-groomed (3) boring (4) discouraged (5) uncertain
2. *atrocious* — (1) brutal (2) innocent (3) shrunken (4) yellowish (5) unsound
3. *blithe* — (1) wicked (2) criminal (3) merry (4) unintelligible (5) substantial
4. *prestige* — (1) speed (2) influence (3) omen (4) pride (5) excuse
5. *trite* — (1) brilliant (2) unusual (3) funny (4) stiff (5) commonplace
6. *vindicate* — (1) outrage (2) waver (3) enliven (4) justify (5) fuse
7. *exude* — (1) accuse (2) discharge (3) inflect (4) appropriate (5) distress
8. *livid* — (1) burned (2) patient (3) hurt (4) salted (5) discolored
9. *faction* — (1) clique (2) judgment (3) truth (4) type of architecture (5) health
10. *inclement* — (1) merciful (2) sloping (3) harsh (4) disastrous (5) personal

TEST SEVEN

1. *commend* — (1) begin (2) praise (3) remark (4) graduate (5) plead

2. *placid* — (1) public (2) watered (3) quiet (4) established (5) colorless

3. *segregate* — (1) multiply (2) encircle (3) conform (4) isolate (5) deny

4. *deride* — (1) plead (2) mock (3) appeal (4) surprise (5) obligate

5. *guile* — (1) blame (2) market (3) direction (4) deceit (5) throat

6. *prudent* — (1) critical (2) cautious (3) bluish (4) unfinished (5) outrageous

7. *ornate* — (1) proper (2) insincere (3) stubborn (4) birdlike (5) adorned

8. *disdainful* — (1) scornful (2) disgraceful (3) willful (4) ungrateful (5) unhealthful

9. *purge* — (1) knit (2) chase (3) pucker (4) elope (5) cleanse

10. *aggravate* — (1) accuse (2) consider (3) grieve (4) intensify (5) engrave

TEST EIGHT

1. *deadlock* — (1) useless material (2) fatigue (3) will (4) fixed limit (5) state of inaction

2. *deputy* — (1) arranger (2) detective (3) fugitive (4) substitute (5) cleanser

3. *oppress* — (1) conclude (2) crush (3) branch out (4) alter (5) stay within

4. *revelation* — (1) respect (2) disclosure (3) repetition (4) suitability (5) remainder

5. *irksome* — (1) unreasonable (2) unclean (3) related (4) aglow (5) tedious

6. *sallow* — (1) yellowish (2) external (3) healing (4) quiet (5) vague

7. *imperious* — (1) large (2) surprising (3) overbearing (4) mischievous (5) healthy

8. *stringent* — (1) rigid (2) threaded (3) musty (4) obtainable (5) avoided

9. *attribute* — (1) characteristic (2) donation (3) friction (4) vengeance (5) dress

10. *wrangle* — (1) dispute (2) come to grips (3) squirm (4) expel moisture (5) plead

TEST NINE

1. *accelerate* — (1) surpass   (2) cheer   (3) quicken   (4) impede   (5) transport
2. *fraudulent* — (1) deceptive   (2) erosive   (3) horrifying   (4) demanding   (5) joking
3. *humdrum* — (1) monotonous   (2) noisy   (3) misleading   (4) distinguished   (5) moist
4. *lethal* — (1) belated   (2) deadly   (3) neglectful   (4) devout   (5) oblivious
5. *impair* — (1) consume   (2) control   (3) design   (4) damage   (5) restrain
6. *ovation* — (1) eggshell   (2) circumference (3) opening   (4) slyness   (5) homage
7. *ravage* — (1) lay waste   (2) complain   (3) talk wildly   (4) rush about   (5) admire
8. *ensue* — (1) ascertain   (2) follow   (3) trap   (4) envelop   (5) plead
9. *detachment* — (1) liking   (2) chance   (3) activity   (4) secrecy   (5) aloofness
10. *caricature* — (1) famine   (2) exaggeration   (3) list   (4) consideration   (5) expense

TEST TEN

1. *intricate* — (1) complicated   (2) fascinating   (3) medium   (4) human   (5) original
2. *genial* — (1) particular   (2) difficult   (3) imaginary   (4) oversized   (5) cheerful
3. *evasive* — (1) penetrating   (2) blotting   (3) shifty   (4) broad   (5) unsympathetic
4. *pomp* — (1) magnificence   (2) aid   (3) thoughtfulness   (4) timeliness   (5) scarcity
5. *phase* — (1) expression   (2) concern   (3) adolescence   (4) aspect   (5) embarrassment
6. *assertion* — (1) declaration   (2) abandonment   (3) agreement   (4) decoding   (5) appraisal
7. *denounce* — (1) abdicate   (2) accuse   (3) execute   (4) displace   (5) recite
8. *exonerate* — (1) free from blame   (2) object   (3) expel   (4) prepare for action   (5) meet secretly
9. *jostle* — (1) entertain   (2) travel afar   (3) crowd   (4) ride horseback   (5) deceive
10. *prerogative* — (1) privilege   (2) inferiority   (3) redemption   (4) **naval command**   (5) **combination**

TEST ELEVEN

1. *immunity* — (1) disease (2) publicity (3) mercy (4) changeableness (5) freedom
2. *posterity* — (1) ancestors (2) ownership (3) amendment (4) descendants (5) fellow-citizens
3. *arrogance* — (1) firmness (2) greatness (3) haughtiness (4) surprise (5) helpfulness
4. *relish* — (1) destroy (2) uphold (3) defy (4) associate (5) enjoy
5. *enmesh* — (1) entangle (2) oppose (3) organize (4) challenge (5) respond
6. *vivacious* — (1) wild (2) erratic (3) disloyal (4) lively (5) direct
7. *deft* — (1) skillful (2) wise (3) particular (4) awkward (5) disagreeable
8. *coalition* — (1) conference (2) election (3) union (4) criticism (5) fueling
9. *exploit* — (1) declaration (2) deed (3) ambition (4) outrage (5) conspiracy
10. *garrulous* — (1) dissipated (2) interwoven (3) military (4) talkative (5) variegated

TEST TWELVE

1. *onslaught* — (1) waste (2) ambition (3) crime (4) attack (5) forgiveness
2. *scrutinize* — (1) examine closely (2) praise openly (3) drink (4) tighten (5) write freely
3. *impartial* — (1) favorite (2) just (3) selfish (4) difficult (5) meaningless
4. *dexterous* — (1) divided (2) harsh (3) individual (4) skillful (5) evil
5. *cardiac* — (1) mental (2) circulatory (3) heart (4) tender (5) crimson
6. *instigate* — (1) uphold (2) conceal (3) accuse (4) renew (5) provoke
7. *rescind* — (1) cancel (2) renew (3) divide (4) pave (5) demand
8. *import* — (1) security (2) denial (3) meaning (4) mission (5) injustice
9. *maudlin* — (1) humorous (2) weakly sentimental (3) pictorial (4) oddly shaped (5) closely related
10. *volition* — (1) electrical power (2) brute strength (3) quantity (4) will (5) large print

TEST THIRTEEN

1. *condole* — (1) apportion   (2) disregard   (3) sympathize   (4) thank   (5) write

2. *chaotic* — (1) unhappy   (2) confused   (3) wrong   (4) deep   (5) unusual

3. *irate* — (1) angry   (2) brave   (3) harmless   (4) responsive   (5) imperturbable

4. *appraisal* — (1) discrimination   (2) distinction   (3) condemnation   (4) respect   (5) valuation

5. *initiate* — (1) begin   (2) overlook   (3) criticize   (4) supervise   (5) commend

6. *insurgent* — (1) headlong   (2) flattering   (3) murderous   (4) rebellious   (5) successful

7. *tremulous* — (1) heavy   (2) large   (3) modern   (4) sickly   (5) quivering

8. *transitory* — (1) pleasant   (2) fleeting   (3) imaginary   (4) memorable   (5) solid

9. *celerity* — (1) neatness   (2) fame   (3) speed   (4) truthfulness   (5) vigor

10. *facade* — (1) front   (2) gate   (3) inner court   (4) Moorish arch   (5) temple

TEST FOURTEEN

1. *abridge* — (1) dilate   (2) shorten   (3) go over   (4) build   (5) connect

2. *humid* — (1) funny   (2) hot   (3) kindly   (4) moist   (5) normal

3. *stabilize* — (1) fasten   (2) pick   (3) steady   (4) succor   (5) vary

4. *pensive* — (1) awkward   (2) declining   (3) iridescent   (4) thoughtful   (5) thwarted

5. *allot* — (1) apportion   (2) economize   (3) offer   (4) permit   (5) restrict

6. *impeach* — (1) accuse   (2) convict   (3) sear   (4) pierce   (5) preserve

7. *glib* — (1) cheerful   (2) fluent   (3) delightful   (4) dull   (5) gloomy

8. *prevaricate* — (1) hesitate   (2) remain silent   (3) protest   (4) delay   (5) lie

9. *utilitarian* — (1) extreme   (2) necessary   (3) perfect   (4) practical   (5) visionary

10. *jargon* — (1) colloquialism   (2) blunt language   (3) slang   (4) idiomatic speech   (5) confused talk

TEST FIFTEEN

1. *dilemma* — (1) quarrel (2) denial (3) predicament (4) apparition (5) embarrassment
2. *apportioned* — (1) collected (2) saved (3) changed (4) distributed (5) accumulated
3. *writhe* — (1) slip (2) sob (3) relax (4) resist (5) squirm
4. *callous* — (1) flowerlike (2) harmful (3) pale (4) unfeeling (5) warm
5. *mediocre* — (1) ordinary (2) confused (3) skillful (4) distraught (5) self-satisfied
6. *rudiment* — (1) beginning (2) refinement (3) nature (4) supposition (5) barbarian
7. *apathy* — (1) illness (2) indolence (3) by-way (4) indifference (5) frailty
8. *invariable* — (1) diverse (2) without end (3) fleeting (4) inescapable (5) uniform
9. *consensus* — (1) general agreement (2) classified group (3) count of people (4) poll of opinion (5) popular scheme
10. *annals* — (1) columns (2) gossip (3) history (4) notations (5) treasure

TEST SIXTEEN

1. *fictitious* — (1) difficult (2) imaginary (3) novel (4) ordinary (5) unknown
2. *methodically* — (1) calmly (2) carelessly (3) openly (4) vigorously (5) systematically
3. *ingenious* — (1) naive (2) crafty (3) insipid (4) clever (5) sincere
4. *proximity* — (1) absence (2) mildness (3) nearness (4) threat (5) appropriateness
5. *siphon* — (1) draw off (2) purify (3) sip (4) soak up (5) wash
6. *futile* — (1) conventional (2) ineffectual (3) meager (4) tardy (5) tedious
7. *hyperbole* — (1) allusion (2) analogy (3) exaggeration (4) humor (5) forcefulness
8. *intern* — (1) detain (2) disarm (3) exchange (4) mistreat (5) search
9. *fluctuate* — (1) bloom (2) evaporate (3) flounder (4) flow upward (5) vary
10. *categorical* — (1) absolute (2) angry (3) false (4) uncertain (5) hasty

TEST SEVENTEEN

1. *antidote* — (1) cure-all   (2) diet   (3) laxative   (4) remedy   (5) salve
2. *reciprocal* — (1) average   (2) cognizant   (3) extended   (4) mutual   (5) uncommon
3. *divulge* — (1) hide   (2) muddle   (3) reveal   (4) suspect   (5) understand
4. *consolidate* — (1) close   (2) fasten   (3) freeze   (4 liquidate   (5) unite
5. *incoherent* — (1) brief   (2) disconnected   (3) exaggerated   (4) hasty   (5) inadequate
6. *ravenous* — (1) clamorous   (2) greedy   (3) insane   (4) rude   (5) startling
7. *vacillating* — (1) consistent   (2) planned   (3) thoughtful   (4) vague   (5) wavering
8. *reiterate* — (1) deny   (2) explain   (3) repeat   (4) retract   (5) state
9. *ostracize* — (1) criticize   (2) discharge   (3) banish   (4) reprimand   (5) slander
10. *intrinsic* — (1) apparent   (2) inherent   (3) financial   (4) usual   (5) ornamental

TEST EIGHTEEN

1. *affiliate* — (1) associate   (2) begin   (3) communicate   (4) compare   (5) compete
2. *deflate* — (1) decorate   (2) destroy   (3) expand   (4) peel   (5) reduce
3. *nonchalant* — (1) ignoble   (2) inoffensive   (3) mentally unsound   (4) undecided   (5) unruffled
4. *desperate* — (1) merciless   (2) quarrelsome   (3) rash   (4) thunderstruck   (5) vigorous
5. *tycoon* – (1) blusterer   (2) bureaucrat   (3) industrial magnate   (4) diplomat   (5) strikebreaker
6. *caustic* — (1) desultory   (2) fallacious   (3) reasonable   (4) stinging   (5) wearing
7. *cache* — (1) box   (2) cave   (3) hiding place   (4) rest room   (5) wagon
8. *astute* — (1) futile   (2) potent   (3) provocative   (4) ruthless   (5) shrewd
9. *awry* — (1) askew   (2) deplorable   (3) odd   (4) simple   (5) striking
10. *cruet* — (1) bottle   (2) cake   (3) napkin   (4) plate   (5) salad

TEST NINETEEN

1. *versatile* — (1) all-round (2) awkward (3) poetic (4) unusual (5) wasteful
2. *dormant* — (1) agile (2) inactive (3) docile (4) profound (5) unsocial
3. *proxy* — (1) agent (2) lawyer (3) promoter (4) referee (5) local magistrate
4. *aptitude* — (1) height (2) donation (3) feeling (4) ability (5) knowledge
5. *deluge* — (1) flood (2) loss (3) support '4) sympathy (5) trouble
6. *fortitude* — (1) completion (2) misfortune (3) pluck (4) success (5) truthfulness
7. *sheath* — (1) belt (2) clothing (3) hook (4) linen (5) scabbard
8. *electorate* — (1) nominee (2) office holder (3) group of voters (4) privileged class (5) defeated candidate
9. *approximation* — (1) amplitude (2) annuity (3) antecedent (4) approach (5) accumulation
10. *adroit* — (1) allergic (2) hostile (3) pompous (4) serene (5) skillful

TEST TWENTY

1. *skepticism* — (1) awe (2) education (3) displeasure (4) opinion (5) doubt
2. *detour* — (1) swear (2) go around (3) wreck (4) let slip (5) turn back
3. *crucial* — (1) painful (2) difficult (3) decisive (4) negligible (5) irritable
4. *calculate* — (1) compute (2) expect (3) investigate (4) multiply (5) specify
5. *espionage* — (1) perfidy (2) sabotage (3) spying (4) sedition (5) treachery
6. *amalgamate* — (1) confuse (2) disband (3) produce (4) unite (5) victimize
7. *hypothesis* — (1) proof (2) assumption (3) estimate (4) random guess (5) established truth
8. *incalculable* — (1) boundless (2) frugal (3) incompetent (4) non-essential (5) unreasonable
9. *cajole* — (1) banter (2) fondle (3) compliment (4) mislead (5) coax
10. *condiment* — (1) ledger (2) ore (3) telegraph device (4) spice (5) musical instrument